Andrew S.

Perl 6

at a Glance

Thanks Albert for your interest in Perl 6!

8 Sep 2018
Bern CH

DeepText — 2017

Perl 6 at a Glance

This book is about Perl 6, a programming language of the Perl family. It covers many basic and in-depth topics of the language and provides the initial knowledge you need to start working with Perl 6. The book does not require any previous experience with Perl, although some general understanding of programming is assumed.

First published in English in January 2017

First published in Russian as a series of articles in the *Pragmatic Perl* magazine in 2014–2015, www.pragmaticperl.com

Published by DeepText, Amsterdam
www.deeptext.media

ISBN 978-90-821568-3-6

Foreword

Perl 6 is a programming language that emerged in 2000. In December 2015, the stable version 6.c of the language specification was released.

This book is the first one based on the stable version. It is intended to allow a quick dive into Perl 6 and is dedicated to those readers who are already familiar with Perl 5 as well as for those who have never used any Perl before.

If you want to follow the examples in the book and test your own programmes, download the Rakudo Star compiler from rakudo.org.

Contents

Chapter 1

Perl 6 Essentials

Chapter 2

Operators

Chapter 3

Code Organization

Chapter 4

Classes

Chapter 5

New Concepts

Chapter 6
Regexes and Grammars

Appendix

Chapter 1
Perl 6 Essentials

Hello, World!

The Perl 6 compiler can either read a programme from a file or from the content of the -e command line switch. The simplest "Hello, World!" programme looks like this:

```
say "Hello, Perl 6!";
```

Save it in a file and run:

```
$ perl6 hello.pl
Hello, Perl 6!
```

Alternatively, you may use the -e option:

```
$ perl6 -e'say "Hello, Perl 6!"'
Hello, Perl 6!
```

Variables

Sigils

Perl 6 uses *sigils* to mark variables. The sigils are partially compatible with the Perl 5 syntax. For instance, scalars, lists and hashes use, respectively, the $, @, and % sigils.

```
my $scalar = 42;
say $scalar;
```

It's not a surprise that the code prints 42.

Consider the following fragment, which also gives a predictable result (the square brackets indicate an array):

```
my @array = (10, 20, 30);
say @array;  # [10 20 30]
```

Now, let's use the advantages of Perl 6 and rewrite the above code, using less typing, both fewer characters and less punctuation:

```
my @list1 = <10 20 30>;
```

Or even like this:

```
my @list2 = 10, 20, 30;
```

Similarly, we can omit parenthesis when initializing a hash, leaving the bare content:

```
my %hash =
    'Language' => 'Perl',
    'Version'  => '6';
say %hash;
```

This small programme prints this (the order of the hash keys in the output may be different, and you should not rely on it):

```
{Language => Perl, Version => 6}
```

To access the elements of a list or a hash, Perl 6 uses brackets of different types. It is important to remember that the sigil always remains the same. In the following examples, we extract a scalar out of a list and a hash:

```
my @squares = 0, 1, 4, 9, 14, 25;
say @squares[3];  # This prints the 4th element, thus 9
```

```
my %capitals =
    'France'  => 'Paris',
    'Germany' => 'Berlin';

say %capitals{'Germany'};
```

An alternative syntax exists for both creating a hash and for accessing its elements. To understand how it works, examine the next piece of code:

```
my %month-abbrs =
    :jan('January'),
    :feb('February'),
    :mar('March');
say %month-abbrs<mar>;  # prints March
```

Naming a variable is a rather interesting thing as Perl 6 allows not only ASCII letters, numbers, and the underscore character but also lots of the UTF-8 elements, including the hyphen and apostrophe:

```
my $hello-world = "Hello, World";
say $hello-world;

my $don't = "Isn't it a Hello?";
say $don't;

my $привет = "A Cyrillic Hi!";
say $привет;
```

Would you prefer non-Latin characters in the names of the variables? Although it may slow down the speed of your typing, because it will require switching the keyboard layout, using non-Latin characters in names of variables does not have any performance impact. But if you do, always think of those developers, who may need to read your code in the future.

Introspection

Due to the mechanism of introspection, it is easily possible to tell the type of the data living in a variable (a variable in Perl 6 is often referred as a *container*). To do that, call the predefined **WHAT** method on a variable. Even if it is a bare scalar, Perl 6 treats it internally as an object; thus, you may call some methods on it.

For scalars, the result depends on the real type of data residing in a variable. Here is an example (parentheses are part of the output):

```
my $scalar = 42;
my $hello-world = "Hello, World";

say $scalar.WHAT;        # (Int)
say $hello-world.WHAT;   # (Str)
```

For those variables, whose names start with the sigils @ and %, the WHAT method returns the strings (Array) and (Hash).

Try with arrays:

```
my @list = 10, 20, 30;
my @squares = 0, 1, 4, 9, 14, 25;

say @list.WHAT;        # (Array)
say @squares.WHAT;     # (Array)
```

Now with hashes:

```
my %hash = 'Language' => 'Perl';
my %capitals = 'France' => 'Paris';

say %hash.WHAT;          # (Hash)
say %capitals.WHAT;      # (Hash)
```

The thing, which is returned after a WHAT call, is a so-called *type object*. In Perl 6, you should use the === operator to compare these objects.

For instance:

```
my $value = 42;
say "OK" if $value.WHAT === Int;
```

There's an alternative way to check the type of an object residing in a container — the isa method. Call it on an object, passing the type name as an argument, and get the answer:

```
my $value = 42;
say "OK" if $value.isa(Int);
```

Twigils

In Perl 6, a variable name may be preceded by either a single-character sigil, such as $, @ or %, or with a double character sequence. In the latter case, this is called a *twigil*. The first character of it means the same thing that a bare sigil does, while the second one extends the description.

For example, the second character of the twigil can describe the scope of the variable. Consider *, which symbolises *dynamic scope* (more on this in Chapter 3). The following call prints the command line arguments one by one:

```
.say for @*ARGS;
```

Here, the @*ARGS array is a global array containing the arguments received from the command line (note that this is called ARGS and not ARGV as in Perl 5). The .say construction is a call of the say method on a loop variable. If you want to make it more verbose, you would write it like this:

```
for @*ARGS {
    $_.say;
}
```

Let's list a few other useful predefined dynamic variables with the star in their twigils. The first element of the twigil denotes the type of a container (thus a scalar, an array, or a hash):

$*PERL contains the Perl version (Perl 6)

$*PID — process identifier

$*PROGRAM-NAME — the name of the file with the currently executing programme (for a one-liner its value is set to -e)

$*EXECUTABLE — the path to the interpreter

$*VM — the name of the virtual machine, which your Perl 6 has been compiled with

$*DISTRO — the name and the version of the operation system distribution

$*KERNEL — similar, but for the kernel

$*CWD — the current working directory

$*TZ — the current timezone

%*ENV — the environment variables

In my case, the variables above took the following values:

```
Perl 6 (6.c)
90177
twigil-vars.pl
"/usr/bin/perl6".IO
moar (2016.11)
macosx (10.10.5)
darwin (14.5.0)
"/Users/ash/Books/Perl 6/code".IO
{Apple_PubSub_Socket_Render => /private/tmp/com.apple....,
DISPLAY => /private/tmp/com.apple..., HISTCONTROL => ig-
norespace, HOME => /Users/ash, LC_CTYPE => UTF-8, LOGNAME
=> ash ...
```

The next group of the predefined variables include those with the ? character as their twigil. These are "constants" or so-called *compile-time constants*, which contain information about the current position of the programme flow.

$?FILE — the name of the file with a programme (no path included; contains the string -e for one-liners)

$?LINE — the line number (is set to 1 for one-liners)

$?PACKAGE — the name of the current module; on a top level, this is (GLOBAL)

$?TABSTOP — the number of spaces in tabs (might be used in *heredocs*)

Frequently used special variables

The $_ variable is the one similar to that in Perl 5, which is the default variable containing the current context argument in some cases. Like any other variable, the $_ is an object in Perl 6, even in the simplest use cases. For example, the recent example .say for @*ARGS implicitly contains the $_.say call. The same effect would give $_.say(), .say(), or just .say.

This variable is used as a default variable in other cases, for instance, during the match against regular expressions:

```
for @*ARGS {
    .say if /\d/;
}
```

This short code is equivalent to the following, which uses the *smart-match* (~~) operator:

```
for @*ARGS {
    $_.say if $_ ~~ /\d/;
}
```

The result of matching against a regular expression is available in the $/ variable. To get the matched string, you may call the $/.Str method. So as to get the substrings, which were caught during the match, indices are used: $/[2] or, in a simpler form, $2.

```
"Perl's Birthday: 18 December 1987" ~~
    / (\d+) \s (\D+) \s (\d+) /;
say $/.Str;
say $/[$_] for 0..2;
```

Here, we are looking for a date. In this case, the date is defined as a sequence of digits \d+, a space \s, the word having no digits \D+, another space \s, and some more digits \d+. If the match succeeded, the $/.Str slot contains the whole date, while the $/[0], $/[1], and $/[2] keep their parts (the small square corner brackets are part of the output to indicate the Match object, see Chapter 6):

```
18 December 1987
⌜18⌟
⌜December⌟
⌜1987⌟
```

Finally, the $! variable will contain an error message, for example, the one that occurred within a try block, or the one that happened while opening a file:

```
try {
    say 42/0;
}
say $! if $!;
```

If you remove the last line in this programme, nothing will be printed. This is because the try block masks any error output. Remove the try, and the error message reappears (the programme, itself, is terminated).

Built-in types

Perl 6 allows using typed variables. To tell the compiler that the variable is typed, you simply need to name the type while declaring the variable.

Some of the types available in Perl 6 are obvious and do not need comments:

```
Bool, Int, Str
Array, Hash, Complex
```

Some might require a small comment:

```
Num, Pair, Rat
```

The `Num` type is used to handle floating-point variables, and a `Pair` is a "key; value" pair. The `Rat` type introduces rational numbers with numerators and denominators.

Typed variables

This is how you declare a typed variable:

```
my Int $x;
```

Here, a scalar container `$x` may only hold an integer value. Attempts to assign it a value that is not an integer leads to an error:

```
my Int $x;
$x = "abc";  # Error: Type check failed in assignment to '$x';
             # expected 'Int' but got 'Str'
```

For typecasts, a respective method call is quite handy. Remember that while `$x` holds an integer, it is treated as a container object as a whole, which is why you may use some predefined methods on it. The same you can do directly on a string. For example:

```
my Int $x;
$x = "123".Int;  # Now this is OK
say $x; # 123
```

Bool

The usage of the `Bool` variables is straightforward although there are some details about which you might want to know. The Bool type is a built-in enumeration and provides two values: `True` and `False` (or, in a full form, `Bool::True` and `Bool::False`). It is permissible to increment or decrement the Boolean variables:

```
my $b = Bool::True;
```

```
$b--;
say $b; # prints False

$b = Bool::False;
$b++;
say $b; # True
```

The Perl 6 objects (namely, all variables) contain the Bool method, which converts the value of the variable to one of the two Boolean values:

```
say 42.Bool; # True

my $pi = 3.14;
say $pi.Bool; # True

say 0.Bool;     # False
say "00".Bool; # True
```

Similarly, you may call the Int method on a variable and get the integer representation of the Boolean values (or values of any other types):

```
say Bool::True.Int; # 1
```

Int

The Int type is intended to host integer variables of arbitrary size. For example, no digit is lost in the following assignment:

```
my Int $x =
    12389147319583948275874801735817503285431532;
say $x;
```

A special syntax exists for defining integers with an other-than-10 base:

```
say :16<D0CF11E0>
```

Also, it is allowable to use the underscore character to separate digits so that big numbers can be read more easily:

```
my Int $x = 735_817_503_285_431_532;
```

Of course, when you print the value, all the underscores are gone.

On the `Int` object, you may call some other handy methods, for example, to convert a number to a character or to check if the integer in hand is prime (yes, `is-prime` is a built-in method!).

```
my Int $a = 65;
say $a.chr;  # A

my Int $i = 17;
say $i.is-prime;  # True

say 42.is-prime;  # False
```

Str

`Str` is no doubt a string. In Perl 6, there are methods to manipulate strings. Again, you call them as methods on objects.

```
my $str = "My string";

say $str.lc;  # my string
say $str.uc;  # MY STRING

say $str.index('t');  # 4
```

Let us now get the length of a string. The naïve attempt to write `$str.length` produces an error message. However, a hint is also provided:

```
No such method 'length' for invocant of type 'Str'
Did you mean 'elems', 'chars', 'graphs' or 'codes'?
```

Thus, we have a simple and a mono-semantic method to get the length of a Unicode string.

```
say "περλ 6".chars;  # 6
```

Getting used to the new way of working with strings as objects may take some time. For example, this how you can call the `printf` as a method on a string:

```
"Today is %02i %s %i\n".printf($day, $month, $year);
```

Array

The `Array` variables (i.e., all the variables starting with the @ sigil) are equipped with a couple of simple but rather useful methods.

```
my @a = 1, 2, 3, 5, 7, 11;
say @a.Int;  # array length
say @a.Str;  # space-separated values
```

If you print an array, you get its value as a space-separated list in square brackets. Alternatively, you may interpolate it in a string.

```
my @a = 1, 2, 3, 5, 7, 11;

say @a;                    # [1 2 3 5 7 11]
say "This is @a: @a[]";    # This is @a: 1 2 3 5 7 11
```

Hash

Hashes provide a few methods with clear semantics, for instance:

```
my %hash = Language => 'Perl', Version => 6;

say %hash.elems;   # number of pairs in the hash
say %hash.keys;    # the list of the keys
say %hash.values;  # the list of the values
```

Here's the output:

```
2
(Version Language)
(6 Perl)
```

It is possible to iterate not only over the hash keys or values but also over whole pairs:

```
for %hash.pairs {
    say $_.key;
    say $_.value;
}
```

The `.kv` method returns a list containing the alternating keys and values of the hash:

```
say %hash.kv  # (Version 6 Language Perl)
```

Chapter 2
Operators

The meanings of the many of the operators in Perl 6 are quite obvious even for those who are not familiar with Perl 5. On the other hand, sometimes the behaviour of the operator contains some tiny details that you may not think of. In this chapter, we will list some operators, giving some comments when it is necessary.

The operators can be divided into a few groups depending on their syntactical properties. These groups are prefixes, infixes, postfixes, and some other types of operators that are not covered here (such as circumflex, which is the "hamburger" operator, like a pair of braces).

Prefixes

Prefix operators are those that come in front of their operands. Obviously, prefix operators require only one operand. In some cases, the symbol of the operation can be used as an infix operator when it stands between two operands.

!, not
! is the Boolean negation operator.

```
say !True;      # False
say !(1 == 2);  # True
```

The not operator does the same but has lower precedence.

```
say not False;  # True
```

+
+ is the unary plus operator, which casts its operand to the numerical context. The action is equivalent to the call of the Numeric method.

```
my Str $price = '4' ~ '2';
my Int $amount = +$price;
```

```
say $amount;          # 42
say $price.Numeric;   # 42
```

We will see one of the important use cases of the unary plus in Chapter 6: +$/. That construction converts an object of the Match class that contains information about the matched part of the regular expression into a number.

—

- is a unary minus, which changes the sign of its operand. Because this operator silently calls the Numeric method, it can also cast the context, as it does the unary plus operator.

```
my Str $price = '4' ~ '2';
say -$price; # -42
```

?, so

? is a unary operator casting the context to a Boolean one by calling the Bool method on an object.

```
say ?42; # True
```

The second form, so, is a unary operator with lower precedence.

```
say so 42;    # True
say so True;  # True
say so 0.0;   # False
```

~

~ casts an object to a string. Note that we are now talking about the prefix or a unary operator. If the tilde is used as an infix (see later in this chapter about what infixes are), it works as a string concatenating operator, but it still deals with strings.

```
```

```
my Str $a = ~42;
say $a.WHAT; # (Str)
```

In some cases, the string context can be created implicitly, for example, when you interpolate a variable inside the double quotes.

++

++ is a prefix operator of increment. First, an increment is done, and then a new value is returned.

```
my $x = 41;
say ++$x; # 42
```

The increment operation is not limited to working only with numbers. It can also handle strings.

```
my $a = 'a';
say ++$a; # b
```

A practical example is to increment filenames containing numbers. The file extension will survive, and only the numerical part will be incremented.

```
my $f = "file001.txt";

++$f;
say $f; # file002.txt

++$f;
say $f; # file003.txt
```

--

-- is a prefix form of decrement. It works exactly like the ++ prefix but, of course, makes the operand smaller (whether it be a string or a number).

```
my $x = 42;
say --$x; # 41
```

28

+^

+^ is a bitwise negation operator with two's complement.

```
my $x = 10;
my $y = +^$x;
say $y;  # -11 (but not -10)
```

Compare this operator with the following one.

?^

?^ is a logical negation operator. Please note that this is not a bitwise negation. First, the argument is converted to a Boolean value, and then the result is negated.

```
my $x = 10;
my $y = ?^$x;
say $y;          # False
say $y.WHAT;     # (Bool)
```

^

^ is a range-creating operator or the so-called *upto* operator. It creates a range (which is an object of the **Range** type) from 0 up to the given value (not including it).

```
.print for ^5;  # 01234
```

This code is equivalent to the following, where both ends of the range are explicitly specified:

```
.print for 0..4;  # 01234
```

|

| flattens the compound objects into a list. For example, this operator should be used when you pass a list to a subroutine, which expects a list of scalars:

```
sub sum($a, $b) {
    $a + $b
}

my @data = (10, 20);
say sum(|@data);  # 30
```

Without the | operator, the compiler will report an error, because the subroutine expects two scalars and cannot accept an array as an argument:

Calling sum(Positional) will never work with declared signature ($a, $b)

temp

temp creates a temporary variable and restores its value at the end of the scope (like it does the `local` built-in operator in Perl 5).

```
my $x = 'x';
{
    temp $x = 'y';
    say $x;  # y
}
say $x;       # x
```

Compare it with the following operator, `let`.

let

`let` is a prefix operator, which is similar to `temp`, but works correctly with exceptions. The previous value of the variable will be restored if the scope was left because of the exception.

```
my $var = 'a';
try {
    let $var = 'b';
    die;
}
say $var;  # a
```

30

With a `die`, this example code will print the initial value a. If you comment out the call of a `die`, the effect of the assignment to b will stay, and the variable will contain the value b after the `try` block.

The `let` keyword looks similar to the declarators like `my` and `our`, but it is a prefix operator.

Postfixes

Postfix operators are unary operators placed after their single operand.

++

++ is a postfix increment. The change of the value happens after the current value is used in the expression.

```
my $x = 42;
say $x++;  # 42
say $x;    # 43
```

- -

-- is a postfix decrement.

Both postfix and prefix operators magically know how to deal with numbers in filenames.

```
my $filename = 'file01.txt';
for 1..10 {
    say $filename++;
}
```
This example prints the list of the filenames with incrementing numbers: file01.txt, file02.txt, ... file10.txt.

Method postfixes

There are a few syntactical elements in Perl 6, which start with a dot. These operators might look like a postfix operator, but they all are the forms of the calling a method on an object. Unlike Perl 5, the dot operator does not do any string concatenation.

.

`.method` calls a `method` on a variable. This works with both real objects and with those variables, which are not instances of any class, for example, built-in types like integers.

```
say "0.0".Numeric;  # 0
say 42.Bool;        # True

class C {
    method m() {say "m()"}
}
my $c = C.new;
$c.m(); # m()
```

.=

`.=method` is a mutating call of the `method` on an object. The call `$x.=method` does the same as the more verbose assignment `$x = $x.method`.

In the following example, the `$o` container initially holds an object of the `C` class, but after `$o.=m()`, the value will be replaced with an instance of the `D` class.

```
class D { }

class C {
    method m() {
        return D.new;
    }
}

my $o = C.new;
say $o.WHAT;   # (C)

$o.=m();
say $o.WHAT;   # (D)
```

.^

`.^method` calls a `method` on the object's metaobject. A metaobject is an instance of the `HOW` class and contains some additional information about the object. The following two operations, applied to the `$i` variable, are equivalent and print the list of the methods available for the `Int` variables.

```
my Int $i;
say $i.^methods();
say $i.HOW.methods($i);
```

.?

`.?method` calls a method if it is defined. If the object does not have a method with the given name, `Nil` is returned.

```
class C {
    method m() {'m'}
}

my $c = C.new();
say $c.?m(); # m
say $c.?n(); # Nil
```

.+

`.+method` makes an attempt to call all the methods with the given name on an object. This may be used, for example, when an instance is a part of the hierarchy of objects and its parent also has a method with the same name. More on the classes and class hierarchy in Chapter 4.

```
class A {
    method m($x) {"A::m($x)"}
}
class B is A {
    method m($x) {"B::m($x)"}
}

my $o = B.new;
my @a = $o.+m(7);
say @a;  # Prints [B::m(7) A::m(7)]
```

Here, the `$o` object has the `m` method in both its own class `B` and in its parent class `A`. The `$o.+m(7)` calls both of the methods and puts their results in a list.

If the method is not defined, an exception will be thrown.

.*

`.*method` calls all the methods with the given `method` name and returns a parcel with the results. If the method is not defined, an empty list is returned. In the rest, it behaves like the `.+` operator.

Infix operators

Infix operators are placed in a programme between two operands. The majority of the infix operators are binary, and there is a single ternary operator, which expects three operands.

The simplest example of the binary operator is an addition operator `+`. On the right and left sides it expects two values, for example, two variables: `$a + $b`. It is important to understand that the same symbol or the same sequence of characters may be either an infix or a prefix operator depending on the context. In the example with a plus, the unary counterpart is a unary plus operator, which coerces the operand to a number: `+$str`.

Numerical operators

+, -, *, /

`+`, `-`, `*`, and `/` are the operators executing the corresponding arithmetical operations and do not require any comments. When working with Perl 6, keep in mind that before the operation is executed, the operands will be automatically converted to the `Numeric` type if it is necessary.

%

`%` is the modulo operator returning the remainder of the integer division. The operands are cast to integers first if necessary.

div, mod

`div` is the integer division operator. If the floating point is truncated, the result is rounded to the preceding lower integer.

```
say 10 div 3;   # 3
say -10 div 3;  # 4
```

`mod` is another form of the modulo:

```
say 10 % 3;    # 1
say 10 mod 3;  # 1
```

Unlike the / and % operators, the `div` and `mod` forms do not cast the operands to the numeric value. Compare the following two examples.

```
say 10 % "3"; # 1
```

With a mod operator, an error occurs:

```
say 10 mod "3";

Calling 'infix:<mod>' will never work with argument types
(Int, Str)
Expected any of: :(Real $a, Real $b)
```

To satisfy the requirements, you may make the type conversion explicitly using either the + prefix operator:

```
say 10 mod +"3"; # 1
```

or calling the `.Int` method:

```
say 10 mod "3".Int; # 1
```

%%

%% is the so-called divisibility operator: it tells if the integer division with no remainder is possible for the given pair of operands.

```
say 10 %% 3; # False
say 12 %% 3; # True
```

+&, +|, +^

+&, +|, and +^ are the bitwise operands for the multiplication, addition, and XOR operations. The plus character in the operators suggests that the operands will be converted to the integer type if necessary.

?|, ?&, ?^

?|, ?&, and ?^ cast the operands to the Boolean type (thus the ? in the operator name) and do the logical operations of OR, AND, and XOR.

+<, +>

+< and +> are the left and right shift operators.

```
say 8 +< 2;     # 32
say 1024 +> 8;  # 4
```

gcd

gcd calculates the greatest common denominator of the two integer operands.

```
say 50 gcd 15;  # 5
```

lcm

lcm finds the least common multiple value for the given operands.

```
say 1043 lcm 14;  # 2086
```

==, !=

== and != compare the two Numeric operands. Typecast is executed first if needed.

<, >, <=, >=

<, >, <=, and >= are the operands to compare Numeric values.

<=>

<=> is the operator to compare numbers. It returns the value of the Order type, which can be Order::Less, Order::More, or Order::Same.

String operators

~

~ does the string concatenation. The dot in Perl 6 is now used for dealing with methods; thus, a new operator for the string concatenation was required. The tilde was a good candidate because it is also used in other string-related operators in Perl 6.

```
say "a" ~ "b"; # ab
```

If necessary, the operator converts its operands to the string type.

```
say "N" ~ 1; # N1
say 4 ~ 2;   # 42
```

x

x repeats the string the given number of times.

```
say "A" x 5; # AAAAA
```

Non-string values will be converted to strings before the operation.

```
say 0 x 5; # 0000
```

If the number of repetitions is negative or zero, an empty string is returned.

eq, ne

eq and ne compare strings for equality or non-equality, respectively.

lt, gt, le, ge

lt, gt, le, and ge are the operators for comparing strings: less, more, less or equal, and more or equal. The operands are converted to the string values if necessary.

leg

`leg` tells if is the two strings are equal or the left operand is less or greater than the second one. Its behaviour is similar to what `<=>` does for numbers or what the `cmp` built-in operator does in Perl 5. Like the `cmp` in Perl 6, the `leg` operator returns a value of the `Order` type.

```
say "a" leg "b";          # Less
say "abc" leg "b";        # Less
say "bc" leg "b";         # More
say "abc" leg "ABC".lc;   # Same
```

Before the operation, the operands are converted to strings if necessary.

```
say 42 leg "+42";  # More
say 42 leg "42";   # Same
```

Universal comparison operators

There are a few operators, which can compare both strings and numbers, or even compound objects like pairs.

cmp

`cmp` compares two objects and returns a value of the `Order` type, either `Less`, or `Same`, or `More`.

```
say 2 cmp 2;    # Same
say 2 cmp 2.0;  # Same
say 1 cmp 2;    # Less
say 2 cmp 1;    # More

say "a" cmp "b";          # Less
say "abc" cmp "b";        # Less
say "bc" cmp "b";         # More
say "abc" cmp "ABC".lc;   # Same
```

```
my %a = (a => 1);
my %b = (a => 1);
say %a cmp %b; # Same
```

When the two operands are of different types (for example, one is a number and the other is a string) you have to be careful and think that the compiler may choose from one of the overloaded versions of the cmp operator. Here is the list of them:

```
proto sub infix:<cmp>(Any, Any)
    returns Order:D is assoc<none>

multi sub infix:<cmp>(Any,      Any)
multi sub infix:<cmp>(Real:D,   Real:D)
multi sub infix:<cmp>(Str:D,    Str:D)
multi sub infix:<cmp>(Enum:D,   Enum:D)
multi sub infix:<cmp>(Version:D, Version:D)
```

(The :D in the declarations is not a smiley; this is a trait indicating that the argument must be defined.)

So, when you ask to compare a string to a number, the most probable choice will be the one having the signature with two strings: (Str:D, Str:D). So, both operands will be cast to strings:

```
say "+42" cmp +42; # Less
say ~42 cmp +42;   # Same
```

before, after

before and after are the comparison operators, which work with operands of different types. It returns a Boolean value of either True or False depending on which operand was considered to be ordered earlier or later.

Type coercion is similar to how it happens with the cmp operator. Remember that depending on the data types the comparison of similar-looking strings or numbers may give different results because the strings are compared alphabetically, while the numbers are ordered by their values:

```
say 10 before 2;        # False
say '10' before '2';    # True
say 10 before 20;       # True
say '10' before '20';   # True
```

eqv

eqv is an operator that tests the two operands for equivalence. It returns the True value if the operands are of the same type and contain the same values.

```
my $x = 3;
my $y = 3;
say $x eqv $y;  # True
```

An example with a bit more complex data structures:

```
my @a = (3, 4);
my @b = (3, 4, 5);
@b.pop;
say @a eqv @b;  # True
```

Note that because the integer and the floating-point types are different data types, comparing two equal numbers may give a False result. The same applies to the comparison with a string containing a numeric value.

```
say 42 eqv 42.0;  # False
say 42 eqv "42";  # False
```

It is even trickier when one of the operands is of the Rat value.

```
say 42 eqv 84/2;         # False, 84/2 is Rat
say 42 eqv (84/2).Int;   # True, the value is cast to Int
```

===

=== returns a `True` value if both operands are the same value. Otherwise, it returns `False`. This operator is also known as the value identity operator.

```
class I { }

# Three different instances
my $i = I.new;
my $ii = I.new;
my $iii = I.new;

my @a = ($i, $ii, $iii);
for @a -> $a {
    for @a -> $b {
        say $a === $b;
        # Prints True only when $a and $b are pointing
        # to the same element of the @a array.
    }
}
```

=:=

`=:=` is the operator to check if the operands refer to the same object. A Boolean value is returned. The operator is called the container identity operator.

```
my $x = 42;
my $y := $x;

say $x =:= $y;  # True
say $y =:= $x;  # True
```

~~

`~~` is the *smartmatch* operator. It compares the objects and tries to work correctly with the operands of any type (that is why the operator is called smart).

```
say 42 ~~ 42.0;  # True
say 42 ~~ "42";  # True
```

The result of the smartmatching depends on the operand order.

Consider the following:

```
say "42.0" ~~ 42;  # True
say 42 ~~ "42.0";  # False
```

That behaviour is explained by how the operator works internally. First, it calculates the value of the right-hand side operand; then it calls the ACCEPTS method on it, passing it the variable $_ with a reference to the left-hand side operand. Each data type defines its own variant of the ACCEPTS method. For example, it compares strings in the Str class, and integers in the Int class.

The preceding two examples may be re-written as the following form, where the asymmetry is clearly visible:

```
say 42.ACCEPTS("42.0");  # True
say "42.0".ACCEPTS(42);  # False
```

List operators

xx
xx repeats the list the given number of times.

```
say (1, -1) xx 2;  # ((1 -1) (1 -1))
```

Like the string x operator, the xx operator returns an empty list if the number of repetitions is zero or negative.

Z
Z is the *zip* operator. It mixes the content of its two operands like a zipper does. The operator continues mixing while there are enough data in both operands.

The code

```
@c = @a Z @b;
```

is equivalent to the following:

```
@c = ((@a[0], @b[0]), (@a[1], @b[1]), …);
```

Consider another example:

```
my @a = ^5;  # A range from 0 to 5 (excluding 5)
my @b = 'a' .. 'e';
say @a Z @b;
```

It reveals the internal structure of the object that will be created after the Z operation:

```
((0 a) (1 b) (2 c) (3 d) (4 e))
```

X

X is the cross product operator, which converts the two given lists to a third one containing all the possible combinations of the elements from the original lists.

```
@c = @a X @b;
```

This is the same as the following sequence:

```
@c = ((@a[0], @b[0]), (@a[0], @b[1]), (@a[0], @b[2]), …
(@a[N], @b[0]), (@a[N], @b[1]), … (@a[N], @b[M]));
```

The length of the two operands can be different (they are N and M in the example above).

. . .

... creates a sequence and is called a sequence operator.

```
my @list = 1 ... 10;
```

The operator can also count backwards:

```
my @back = 10 ... 1;
```

Junction operators

|, &, ^

|, &, and ^ create the so-called junctions (formerly known in Perl 6 as quantum superpositions). These objects can be used where a scalar is used but behave differently; unlike the scalars, the junctions have multiple values at the same moment in time.

The |, &, and ^ operators create, respectively, the junctions of the any, all, and one types.

```
# The value of 4 is one of the listed options
say "ok" if 4 == 1|2|3|4|5;
```

```
# There is no 4 in the list
say "ok" if 4 != 1 & 2 & 3 & 5;
```

```
# 4 repeats twice, thus it is not unique
say "ok" unless 4 == 1 ^ 2 ^ 2 ^ 4 ^ 4 ^ 5;
```

Shortcut operators

&&

&& returns the first of the operands, which, after being converted to a Boolean value, becomes False. If none are False, then the last element is returned. Please note that the result is not a Boolean value but the value of one of the operands (unless they are Boolean already).

```
say 10 && 0;  # 0
say 0 && 10;  # 0
say 12 && 3.14 && "" && "abc";  # empty string
```

The operator stops its work as soon as the acceptable value has been found. The values of the rest of the operands will not be calculated. That is why the operator belongs to the group of shortcut operators.

||

|| returns the first operand, which is True in a Boolean context. The remaining operands are not evaluated.

```
say 10 || 0;  # 10
say 0 || 10;  # 10
```

^^

^^ returns an operand that is True in a Boolean context and that is, at the same time, the only one in the given list. If nothing is found, Nil is returned. As soon as the operator sees the second True value, it stops evaluating the rest, because the result is already known.

```
say 0 ^^ '' ^^ "abc" ^^ -0.0;   # abc
say 0 ^^ '' ^^ "abc" ^^ -10.0;  # Nil
```

//

// returns the first defined operand. The operator is called a defined-or operator. It is also is a shortcut operator.

```
my $x;
my $y = 42;
my $z;
say $x // $y // $z;  # 42
```

Other infix operators

min, max

min and max return, correspondently, the minimum and maximum value of their operands.

```
say 20 min 10;        # 10
say 'three' max 'two'; # two (sorted alphabetically)
```

?? !!

?? !! is the ternary operator. It works as its counterpart ? : in Perl 5. The characters are doubled to avoid the mixture with infix operators ? and !, which change the context of their operands.

```
say rand < 0.5 ?? 'Yes' !! 'No';
```

=

= assigns a value to a variable.

=>

=> creates an object of the Pair type. The Pair is a "key; value" combination, like those used in hashes. In the code, it is not always necessary to quote the key values.

```
my $pair = alpha => "one";

my %data = jan => 31, feb => 28, mar => 31;
```

,

, creates a List object. Note that this operator, as a few mentioned above, can be chained to accept more than two operands.

```
my $what = (1, 2, 3);
say $what.WHAT; # (List)
```

The comma is also used as a separator of parameters passed to the subroutine.

To create an empty list, use a pair of parentheses ().

:

: marks the left side of it as an invocant to call a method on, when a method of an object is used. It is easier to understand how it works in the following example.

```
class C {
    method meth($x) {
        say "meth($x)";
    }
}
my $o = C.new;
meth($o: 42);  # The meth method of the $o object is called,
               # it prints "meth(42)"
```

The form meth($o: 42) is equivalent to the classical form $o.meth(42). Note that you cannot omit a space following the colon (otherwise, it will be interpreted as a named argument).

Another common Perl 6 idiom for the use of : is to prevent having parentheses with method calls. The following two lines of code are equivalent:

```
say "abcd".substr: 1, 2; # bc
say "abcd".substr(1, 2); # bc
```

Meta-operators

The design of the operators in Perl 6 is very consistent. For example, if you add a new operator to the language, Perl 6 will create a few more to keep the harmony. In this section, we will talk about the so-called meta-operators, the operators over other operators.

Assignment

The assignment meta-operators (=) use the other operators to create the constructions like +=, ~=, etc. The action of the newly created operators is always equivalent to the verbose code.

If you type $a op= $b, then a compiler will execute the following action: $a = $a op $b.

That means that $x += 2 is equivalent to $x = $x + 2, and $str ~= '.' to $str = $str ~ '.'.

Let us now create a new custom operator and see if the assignment meta-operator will be available for us. On purpose, I chose quite an outstanding-looking operator ^_^:

```
sub infix:<^_^>($a, $b) {
    $a ~ '_' ~ $b
}
```

First, check the simple usage of the new operator with two operands:

```
say 4 ^_^ 5; # 4_5
```

Then, let us try the meta-operator form of it: ^_^=:

```
my $x = 'file';

$x ^_^= 101;
say $x; # file_101
```

Negation

The negating exclamation mark ! is used to create the next set of meta-operators. If it is prepended to the existing operator op, you get the operator that gives you the negated result !op.

```
say "no" if "abcd" !~~ "e";
```

Reverse operator

The prefix R forms the reverse operator for the infix operators, such as / or cmp. The reverse operator does the same as the original but changes the order of the operands.

If necessary, it also changes the operator's associativity. This matters when you have more than two operands in a row. For example, in the code $a op $b $op $c the operators are calculated left to right; that is, first, the value of $a is evaluated. With the reverse operator, the value of $c will be calculated first in the same sequence $a Rop $b Rop $c.

```
say 2 R/ 10;  # 5. Same as say 10 / 2
```

The reverse operators may be very useful together with the reduction operators. Here is an example of how you can reverse and join the values in one go:

```
say [R~] 'a'..'z';  # zyxwvutsrqponmlkjihgfedcba
```

Reduction

For any infix operator op the reduction form [op] also exists. The reduction operator takes a list, enrols its values, and inserts the operator between them.

Examine the example with the [*] reduction operator:

```
[*] 1..5
```

The form above is equivalent to the following line:

```
1 * 2 * 3 * 4 * 5
```

Reduction operators also will be automatically created for the user-defined operators. For example, create the operator that accumulates the sum of every pair of operands that it ever received. Notice the state variable, which works as it does in regular subs, keeping the value between the sub calls.

```
sub infix:<pairsum>($a, $b) {
    state $sum = 0;
    $sum += $a + $b;
}

say [pairsum] 1, 2, 3; # 9
say [pairsum] 1, 2, 3; # 27
```

To understand the result, let's add the debugging output to the operator body:

```
sub infix:<pairsum>($a, $b) {
    state $sum = 0;
    say "[$a + $b]";
    $sum += $a + $b;
}
```

Also note that the function returns the last calculated value; that's why there is no need for an explicit `return $sum` statement.

So, the call of [pairsum] `1, 2, 3` prints the following lines:

```
[1 + 2]
[3 + 3]
```

It is important to realise that the second call receives the values 3 and 3, not 2 and 3 from the original sub call. This is because in the second call, the left operand will contain the previously calculated value, which is also 3 at that moment.

Cross-operators

The cross meta-operator prefix, X, applies an operation to all the possible combinations of the elements of the operands that are treated in list context. The result of the cross-operation is also a list.

Here is an example that prints the coordinates for all the cells of a chess board:

```
say 'a'..'h' X~ 1..8;
```

Zip meta-operators

The zip meta-operator prefix, Z, combines the corresponding elements of its list operands like the zipper does. The record

```
@a Z+ @b
```

is equivalent to this (in Perl 6, the last element of an array is indexed as *-1, not just -1; see the details in Appendix):

```
((@a[0] + @b[0]), (@a[1] + @b[1]), ... (@a[*-1] + @b[*-1]))
```

Notice that the zip meta-operator differs from the Z infix operator. Compare the output of the following test programme:

```
my @a = 1, 2, 3;
my @b = 10, 20, 30;

say @a Z+ @b; # (11 22 33)
say @a Z @b;  # ((1 10) (2 20) (3 30))
```

Here is another example with the => operator, which creates pairs:

```
my @a = ^5;
my @b = 'a' .. 'e';
say @a Z=> @b
```

As you can see, the => operator is used indeed:

```
(0 => a 1 => b 2 => c 3 => d 4 => e)
```

The default operator for Z is comma ,. Thus, @a Z @ b and @a Z, @b produce the same result.

```
my @a = ^5;
my @b = 'a' .. 'e';
say @a Z, @b
```

The output is the same as in the example in the section about list operators earlier in this chapter.

((0 a) (1 b) (2 c) (3 d) (4 e))

Hyper-operators

Hyper-operators modify regular operators in such a way that the operation is applied to all the element of a list operand. Both unary and binary operators may be written in the hyper-operator form. To create a hyper-operator, add a pair of >> and/or << to the operation sign.

Let's start with a simple unary operator !:

```
my @a = (True, False, True);
my @b = !<< @a;
say @b;  # False True False
```

Another example, now with the postfix operator:

```
my @a = (1, 2, 3);
@a>>++;
say @a;  # [2 3 4]
```

In both examples, an operation was applied to each element of the given list. Keep in mind that you should avoid spaces around or inside the hyper-operator because the compiler may be confused otherwise.

```
my @a = ('a', 'b')>>.uc;
# You cannot type ('a', 'b') >>. uc

say @a;  # [A B]
```

Hyper-operators use the angle brackets, and it is possible to make four different combinations and directions of them:

```
>>+>>  <<+<<  <<+>>  >>+<<
```

The direction of the double brackets changes the result of the hyper-operation. If both operands are of the same length, the symmetrical forms work the same:

```
my @a = (1, 2, 3) >>+<< (4, 5, 6);
say @a; # [5 7 9]

my @b = (1, 2, 3) <<+>> (4, 5, 6);
say @b; # [5 7 9]
```

When the lengths of the lists in operands are different, the direction of arrows indicates whether the compiler needs to extend the shortest operand so that there are enough elements to make the operation with all the elements of the longer list.

The simplest case is a combination of a list and a scalar:

```
say((1, 2, 3) >>+>> 1); # (2 3 4)
```

The scalar 1 will be repeated three times.

In the next example, we have two lists, but the second one is shorter.

```
my @a = (1, 2, 3, 4) >>+>> (1, -1);
say @a; # [2 1 4 3]
```

Now, the second list was repeated twice and the left array was in fact added to (1, -1, 1, -1). So as you see, the sharp end of the arrows points to the shorter operand.

If you reverse the order or the operands, you should also change the direction of the hyper-operator:

```
my @b = (1, -1) <<+<< (1, 2, 3, 4);
say @b; # [2 1 4 3]
```

If the list length is not known, use the form of the hyper-operator, where both arrows are pointing outside: <<+>>.

```
my @a = (1, -1) <<+>> (1, 2, 3, 4);
say @a; # [2 1 4 3]
```

```
my @b = (1, 2, 3, 4) <<+>> (1, -1);
say @b; # [2 1 4 3]
```

It is not possible to use the operator >>+<< because it expects that both operands are of the same length, and if they are not, then a runtime error occurs:

Lists on either side of non-dwimmy hyperop of infix:<+> are not of the same length

Finally, it is possible to use non-ASCII characters and use the French quotes instead of the pair of angle brackets:

```
say((1,2) »+« (3,4)); # (4 6)
```

Chapter 3
Code Organization

Subroutines, or subs

For a sub, which takes no arguments, its definition and the call are very straightforward and easy.

```
sub call-me {
    say "I'm called"
}

call-me;
```

The syntax for declaring a sub's parameters is similar to what other languages (including Perl 5.20 and higher) provide.

```
sub cube($x) {
    return $x ** 3;
}

say cube(3);  # 27
```

The required parameters are a comma-separated list in the parentheses immediately after the sub name. No other keywords, such as my, are required to declare them.

```
sub min($x, $y) {
    return $x < $y ?? $x !! $y;
}

say min(-2, 2);   # -2
say min(42, 24);  # 24
```

(?? ... !! is a ternary operator in Perl 6. Also, there's a built-in operator min; see the details in the Chapter 2.)

The above-declared arguments are required; thus, if a sub is called with a different number of actual arguments, an error will occur.

Non-value argument passing

By default, you pass the arguments by their values. Despite that, it is not possible to modify them inside the sub. To pass a variable by reference, add the `is rw` trait. (Note that formally this is not a reference but a mutable argument.)

```
sub inc($x is rw) {
    $x++;
}

my $value = 42;
inc($value);
say $value; # 43
```

Typed arguments

Similarly to the above-described typed variables, it is possible to indicate that the sub's parameters are typed. To do so, add a type name before the name of the parameter.

```
sub say-hi(Str $name) {
    say "Hi, $name!";
}
```

If the types of the expected and the actual parameters do not match, a compile-time error will occur.

```
say-hi("Mr. X"); # OK
```

```
# say-hi(123); # Error: Calling say-hi(Int) will never work
             # with declared signature (Str $name)
```

Optional parameters

Optional parameters are marked with a question mark after their names. The `defined` built-in function helps to tell if the parameter was really passed:

```
sub send-mail(Str $to, Str $bcc?) {
    if defined $bcc {
        # . . .
        say "Sent to $to with a bcc to $bcc.";
    }
    else {
        # . . .
        say "Sent to $to.";
    }
}

send-mail('mail@example.com');
send-mail('mail@example.com', 'copy@example.com');
```

Default values

Perl 6 also allows specifying the default values of the sub's arguments. Syntactically, this looks like an assignment.

```
sub i-live-in(Str $city = "Moscow") {
    say "I live in $city.";
}

i-live-in('Saint Petersburg');
i-live-in(); # The default city
```

It is also possible to pass values that are not known at the compile phase. When the default value is not a constant, it will be calculated at runtime.

```
sub to-pay($salary, $bonus = 100.rand) {
    return ($salary + $bonus).floor;
}

say to-pay(500, 50); # Always 550 net.
say to-pay(500);       # Any number between 500 and 600.
say to-pay(500);       # Same call but probably different output.
```

The "default" value will be calculated whenever it is required. Please also note that both rand and floor are called as methods, not as functions.

60

It is also possible to use previously passed parameters as default values:

```
sub f($a, $b = $a) {
    say $a + $b;
}

f(42);     # 84
f(42, -1) # 41
```

Optional parameters or parameters with default values must be listed after all the required ones because otherwise, the compiler will not be able to understand which is which.

Named arguments

Apart from the positional parameters (those that have to go in the same order both in the sub definition and in the sub call), Perl 6 allows named variables, somewhat similar to how you pass a hash to a Perl 5 subroutine. To declare a named parameter, a semicolon is used:

```
sub power(:$base, :$exponent) {
    return $base ** $exponent;
}
```

Now, the name of the variable is the name of the parameter, and the order is not important anymore.

```
say power(:base(2), :exponent(3)); # 8
say power(:exponent(3), :base(2)); # 8
```

It is also possible to have different names for the named arguments and those variables, which will be used inside the sub. To give a different name, put it after a colon:

```
sub power(:val($base), :pow($exponent)) {
    return $base ** $exponent;
}
```

Now the sub expects new names of the arguments.

```
say power(:val(5), :pow(2)); # 25
say power(:pow(2), :val(5)); # 25
```

Alternatively, you can use the *fatarrow* syntax to pass named parameters as it is done in the following example:

```
say power(val => 5, pow => 2); # 25
```

Slurpy parameters and flattening

Perl 6 allows passing scalars, arrays, hashes, or objects of any other type as the arguments to a sub. There are no restrictions regarding the combination and its order in a sub declaration. For example, the first argument may be an array, and the second one may be a scalar. Perl 6 will pass the array as a whole. Thus the following scalar will not be eaten by the array.

In the following example, the @text variable is used inside the sub, and it contains only the values from the array passed in the sub call.

```
sub cute-output(@text, $before, $after) {
    say $before ~ $_ ~ $after for @text;
}

my @text = <C C++ Perl Go>;
cute-output(@text, '{', '}');
```

The output looks quite predictable.

```
{C}
{C++}
{Perl}
{Go}
```

The language expects that the sub receives the arguments of the same types that were listed in the sub declaration.

That also means, for example, that if the sub is declared with only one list argument, then it cannot accept a few scalars.

```
```

```
sub get-array(@a) {
    say @a;
}

get-array(1, 2, 3);  # Error: Calling get-array(Int, Int, Int)
                     # will never work with declared signature (@a)
```

To let an array accept a list of separate scalar values, you need to say that explicitly by placing an asterisk before the argument name. Such an argument is called *slurpy*.

```
sub get-array(*@a) {
    say @a;
}

get-array(1, 2, 3);  # Good: [1 2 3]
```

Similarly, it will work in the opposite direction, that is to say, when the sub expects to get a few scalars but receives an array when called.

```
sub get-scalars($a, $b, $c) {
    say "$a and $b and $c";
}

my @a = <3 4 5>;
get-scalars(@a);  # Error: Calling get-scalars(Positional)
                  # will never work with declared
                  # signature ($a, $b, $c)
```

A vertical bar is used to unpack an array to a list of scalars.

```
get-scalars(|@a);  # 3 and 4 and 5
```

Nested subs

Nested subs are allowed in Perl 6.

```
sub cube($x) {
    sub square($x) {
        return $x * $x;
    }

    return $x * square($x);
}

say cube(3);  # 27
```

The name of the inner sub `square` is only visible within the body of the outer sub `cube`.

Anonymous subs

Let's look at the creation of anonymous subs. One of the options (there are more than one) is to use syntax similar to what you often see in JavaScript.

```
say sub ($x, $y) {$x ~ ' ' ~ $y}("Perl", 6);
```

The first pair of parentheses contains the list of formal arguments of the anonymous sub; the second, the list of the arguments passed. The body of the sub is located between the braces. (The tilde denotes a string concatenation operator in Perl 6.)

By the way, it is important that there be no spaces before parentheses with the actual values of the sub parameters.

Another way of creating an anonymous sub is to use the arrow operator (`->`). We will discuss it later in the section dedicated to anonymous blocks.

Variables and signatures

Lexical variables

Lexical variables in Perl 6 are those declared with the my keyword. These variables are only visible within the block where they were declared. If you tried accessing them outside the scope, you'd get the error: `Variable '$x' is not declared`.

```
{
    my $x = 42;
    say $x;  # This is fine
}
# say $x;    # This is not
```

To "extend" the scope, lexical variables can be used in closures. In the following example, the seq sub returns a block, which uses a variable defined inside the sub.

```
sub seq($init) {
    my $c = $init;
    return {$c++};
}
```

The sub returns a code block containing the variable $c. After the sub's execution, the variable will not only still exist but also will keep its value, which you can easily see by calling a function by its reference a few times more.

```
my $a = seq(1);

say $a(); # 1
say $a(); # 2
say $a(); # 3
```

It is possible to create two independent copies of the local variable.

```
my $a = seq(1);
my $b = seq(42);
```

To see how it works, call the subs a few times:

```
say $a(); # 1
say $a(); # 2
say $b(); # 42
say $a(); # 3
say $b(); # 43
```

state variables

State variables (declared with the keyword state) appeared in Perl 5.10 and work in Perl 6. Such variables are initialized during the first call and keep their values in subsequent sub calls.

It is important to keep in mind that a single instance of the variable is created. Let us return to the example with a counter and replace the my declaration with the state one. The closure will now contain a reference to the same variable.

```
sub seq($init) {
    state $c = $init;
    return {$c++};
}
```

What happens when you create more than one closure?

```
my $a = seq(1);
my $b = seq(42);
```

All of them will reference the same variable, which will increase after calling either $a() or $b().

```
say $a(); # 1
say $a(); # 2
say $b(); # 3
say $a(); # 4
say $b(); # 5
```

Dynamic variables

The scope of dynamic variables is calculated at the moment when a variable is accessed. Thus, two or more calls of the same code may produce different results.

Dynamic variables are marked with the * twigil (a character clearly referencing a wildcard).

In the following example, the echo() function prints a dynamic variable $*var, which is not declared in the function, nor is it a global variable. It, nevertheless, can be resolved when used in other functions, even if they have their own instances of the variable with the same name.

```
sub alpha {
    my $*var = 'Alpha';
    echo();
}

sub beta {
    my $*var = 'Beta';
    echo();
}

sub echo() {
    say $*var;
}

alpha();  # Alpha
beta();   # Beta
```

Anonymous code blocks

Perl 6 introduces the concept of so-called *pointy blocks* (or pointy arrow blocks). These are anonymous closure blocks, which return a reference to the function and can take arguments.

The syntax of defining pointy blocks is an arrow -> followed by the argument list and a block of code.

```
my $cube = -> $x {$x ** 3};
say $cube(3); # 27
```

Here, the block {$x ** 3}, which takes one argument $x, is created first. Then, it is called using a variable $cube as a reference to the function: $cube(3).

Pointy blocks are quite handy in loops.

```
for 1..10 -> $c {
    say $c;
}
```

The for loop takes two arguments: the range 1..10 and the block of code with the argument $c. The whole construction looks like syntactic sugar for loops.

There can be more than one argument. In that case, list them all after an arrow.

```
my $pow = -> $x, $p {$x ** $p};
say $pow(2, 15); # 32768
```

The same works with loops and with other Perl elements where you need passing anonymous code blocks.

```
for 0..9 -> $i, $j {
    say $i + $j;
}
```

In a loop iteration, two values from the list are consumed each time. So, the loop iterates five times and prints the sum of the pairs of numbers: 1, 5, 9, 13 and 17.

Placeholders

When an anonymous code block is created, declaring a list of arguments is not mandatory even when a block takes an argument. To let this happen, Perl 6 uses special variable containers, which come with the ^ twigil. This is similar to the predefined variables $a and $b in Perl 5.

In the case of more than one argument, their actual order corresponds to the alphabetical order of the names of the ^-ed variables.

```
my $pow = {$^x ** $^y};
say $pow(3, 4); # 81
```

The values 3 and 4, which were passed in the function call, will land in its variables $^x and $^y, respectively.

Now, let us go back to the loop example from the previous section and rewrite it in the form with no arguments (and thus, no arrow).

```
for 0..9 {
    say "$^n2, $^n1";
}
```

Note that the code block starts immediately after the list, and there is no arrow. There are two loop variables, $^n1 and $^n2, and they are not in alphabetical order in the code. Still, they get the values as though they were mentioned in the function signature as ($n1, $n2).

Finally, the placeholders may be named parameters. The difference is in the twigil. To make the placeholder named, use the colon :.

```
my $pow = {$:base ** $:exp};
say $pow(:base(25), :exp(2)); # 625
```

With the named placeholders, the alphabetical order is of no importance anymore. The following call gives us the same result.

```
say $pow(:exp(2), :base(25)); # 625
```

Keep in mind that using named placeholders is just a different way of specifying a signature to the block, and you cannot have both.

The following example demonstrates that you cannot use a placeholder with the name of the already existing parameter:

```
sub f($a) {
    # say $^a; # Error: Redeclaration of symbol '$ ^ a'
              # as a placeholder parameter
}
```

Neither you can use any other placeholder names if the signature of the sub is already defined:

```
sub f($a) {
    say $^b;  # Placeholder variable '$ ^ b' cannot
              # override existing signature
}
```

Function overloading

The `multi` keyword allows defining more than one function (or subroutine, or simply sub) with the same name. The only restriction is that those functions should have different signatures. In Perl 6, the signature of the sub is defined together with its name, and the arguments may be typed. In the case of multi subs, typed arguments make even more sense because they help to distinguish between different versions of the function with a single name and make a correct choice when the compiler needs to call one of them.

```
multi sub twice(Int $x) {
    return $x * 2;
}
multi sub twice(Str $s) {
    return "$s, $s";
}
```

70

```
say twice(42);    # 84
say twice("hi"); # hi, hi
```

As we have two functions here, one taking an integer argument and
another expecting a string, the compiler can easily decide which one it
should use.

Sub overloading with subtypes

Multi subs can be made even more specific by using subtypes. In Perl 6,
subtypes are created with the **subset** keyword. A subtype definition
takes one of the existing types and adds a restriction to select the values to be included in the subtype range.

The following lines give a clear view of how subtypes are defined. From
the same integer type, `Int`, the `Odd` subtype selects only the odd numbers, while the `Even` subtype picks only the even numbers.

```
subset Odd of Int where {$^n % 2 == 1};
subset Even of Int where {$^n % 2 == 0};
```

Now, the subtypes can be used in the signatures of the multi subs. The
`testnum` function has two versions, one for odd and one for even numbers.

```
multi sub testnum(Odd $x) {
    say "$x is odd";
}

multi sub testnum(Even $x) {
    say "$x is even";
}
```

Which function will be used in a call, `testnum($x)`, depends on the
actual value of the variable $x. Here is an example with the loop, calling
either `testnum(Even)` for even numbers or `testnum(Odd)` for odd
numbers.

```
for 1..4 -> $x {
    testnum($x);
}
```

The loop prints a sequence of alternating function call results, which tells us that Perl 6 made a correct choice by using the rules provided in the subtype definitions.

```
1 is odd
2 is even
3 is odd
4 is even
```

Modules

Basically, the Perl 6 modules are the files on disk containing the Perl 6 code. Modules are kept in files with the .pm extension. The disk hierarchy reflects the namespace enclosure, which means that a module named X::Y corresponds to the file X/Y.pm, which will be searched for in one of the predefined catalogues or in the location specified by the -I command line option. Perl 6 has more sophisticated rules for where and how to search for the real files (e. g., it can distinguish between different versions of the same module), but let us skip that for now.

module

The keyword module declares a module. The name of the module is given after the keyword. There are two methods of scoping the module. Either it can be a bare directive in the beginning of a file, or the whole module can be scoped in the code block within the pair of braces.

In the first option, the rest of the file is the module definition (note the presence of the unit keyword).

```
unit module X;

sub x() {
    say "X::x()";
}
```

In the second option, the code looks similar to the way you declare classes (more on classes in Chapter 4).

```
module X {
    sub x() {
        say "X::x()";
    }
}
```

export

The `my` and `our` variables, as well as `subs`, which are defined in the module, are not visible outside of its scope by default. To export a name, the `is export` trait is required.

```
unit module X;

sub x() is export {
    say "X::x()";
}
```

This is all you need to do to be able to call the `x()` sub in the programme using your module.

use

To use a module in your code, use the keyword `use`.

An example. Let us first create the module `Greet` and save it in the file named `Greet.pm`.

```
unit module Greet;

sub hey($name) is export {
    say "Hey, $name!";
}
```

Then, let us use this module in our programme by saying use Greet.

```
use Greet;

hey("you");  # Hey, you!
```

Module names can be more complicated. With is export, all the exported names will be available in the current scope after the module is used.

In the following example, the module Greet::Polite sits in the Greet/Polite.pm file.

```
module Greet::Polite {
    sub hello($name) is export {
        say "Hello, $name!";
    }
}
```

The programme uses both of these modules and can access all the exported subs.

```
use Greet;
use Greet::Polite;

hey("you");       # a sub from Greet
hello("Mr. X");   # from Greet::Polite
```

import

The use keyword automatically imports the names from modules. When a module is defined in the current file in the lexical scope (please note that the module can be declared as local with my module), no import will be done by default. In this case, importing the names should be done explicitly with the `import` keyword.

```
my module M {
    sub f($x) is export {
        return $x;
    }
}

import M;

say f(42);
```

The `f` name will only be available for use after it is imported. Again, only the names marked as `is export` are exported.

As import happens in the compile-time, the `import` instruction itself can be located even after some names from the module are used.

```
my module M {
    sub f($x) is export {
        return $x;
    }
}

say f(1); # 1
import M;
say f(2); # 2
```

need

To just load a module and do no exports, use the **need** keyword.

Let us create a module named **N**, which contains the sub n(). This time, the sub is declared as **our** but with no `is export`.

```
unit module N;

our sub n() {
    say "N::n()";
}
```

Then you **need** a module and may use its methods using the fully quali-
fied names.

```
need N;
```

```
N::n();
```

The sequence of the two instructions: need M; import M; (now import should always come after the **need**) is equivalent to a single **use**
M; statement.

require

The **require** keyword loads a module at a runtime unlike the **use**,
which loads it at the compile-time.

For example, here is a module with a single sub, which returns the sum
of its arguments.

```
unit module Math;
```

```
our sub sum(*@a) {
    return [+] @a;
}
```

(The star in *@a is required to tell Perl to pack all the arguments into a
single array so that we can call the sub as sum(1, 2, 3). With no *, a
syntax error will occur, as the sub expects an array but not three scalars.)

Now, **require** the module and use its sub.

```
require Math;
```

```
say Math::sum(24..42); # 627
```

Before the **import** Math instruction, the programme will not be able to
call Math::sum() because the name is not yet known. A single **import**

`Math;` will not help as the import happens at compile-time when the module is not loaded yet.

Import summary

Here is a concise list of the keywords for working with modules.

`use` loads and imports a module at compile time

`need` loads a module at compile time but does not import anything from it

`import` imports the names from the loaded module at compile time

`require` loads a module at runtime without importing the names

Chapter 4
Classes

We have already seen elements of the object-oriented programming in Perl 6. Methods may be called on those variables, which do not look like real objects from the first view. Even more, methods may be called on constants.

The types that were used earlier (like `Int` or `Str`) are container types. Variables of a container type can contain values corresponding to some native representation. The compiler does all the conversion it needs for executing a programme. For example, when it sees `42.say`, it calls the `say` method, which the `Int` object inherits from the top of the type hierarchy in Perl 6.

Perl 6 also supports object-oriented programming in its general understanding. If you are familiar with how to use classes in other modern programming languages, it will be easy for you to work with classes in Perl 6.

This is how the class is declared:

```
class Cafe {
}
```

Class attributes

Class data variables are called attributes. They are declared with the `has` keyword. An attribute's scope is defined via its twigil. As usual, the first character of the twigil indicates the type of the container (thus, a scalar, an array, or a hash). The second character is either `.` if a variable is public or `!` for the private ones. An *accessor* will be generated by a compiler for the public attributes.

```
class Cafe {
    has $.name;
    has @!orders;
}
```

To create or instantiate an object of the class X, the constructor is called: X.new(). This is basically a method derived from the Any class (this is one of the classes on the top of the object system in Perl 6).

```
my $cafe = Cafe.new(
    name => "Paris"
);
```

At this point, you can read public attributes.

```
say $cafe.name;
```

Reading from $.name is possible because, by default, all public fields are readable and a corresponding access method for them is created. However, that does not allow changing the attribute. To make a field writable, indicate it explicitly by adding the is rw trait.

```
class Cafe {
    has $.name is rw;
    has @!orders;
}

my $cafe = Cafe.new(
    name => "Paris"
);
```

Now, read and write actions are available.

```
$cafe.name = "Berlin";
say $cafe.name;
```

Class methods

The method keyword defines a method, similarly to how we define subroutines with sub. A method has access to all attributes of the class, both public and private.

The method itself can be private. We will return to this later after talking about inheritance.

In the following short example, two methods are created, and each of them manipulates the private @!orders array.

```
class Cafe {
    has $.name;
    has @!orders;

    method order($what) {
        @!orders.push($what);
    }

    method list-orders {
        @!orders.sort.join(', ').say;
    }
}

my $cafe = Cafe.new(
    name => "Paris"
);

$cafe.order('meet');
$cafe.order('fish');
$cafe.list-orders; # fish, meet
```

The code should be quite readable for people familiar with OOP. Just keep in mind that "everything is an object" and you may chain method calls.

```
@!orders.sort.join(', ').say;
```

Instance methods receive a special variable, self (having no sigil), which points to the current object. It can be used to access instance data or the class methods.

```
method order($what) {
    @!orders.push($what);
    self.list-orders;
}

method list-orders {
    say self.name;
    @!orders.sort.join(', ').say;
}
```

Inheritance

Inheritance is easy. Just say `is Baseclass` when declaring a class. Having said that, your class will be derived from the base class.

```
class A {
    method x {
        say "A.x"
    }
    method y {
        say "A.y"
    }
}

class B is A {
    method x {
        say "B.x"
    }
}
```

The further usage of the inherited classes is straightforward.

```
my $a = A.new;
$a.x; # A.x
$a.y; # A.y

my $b = B.new;
$b.x; # B.x
$b.y; # A.y
```

It is important that the result of the method search does not depend on which type was used to declare a variable. Perl 6 always will first use the methods belonging to the class of the variable, which is currently stored in the variable container. For example, return to the previous example and declare the variable $b to be one of type A, but still create an instance of B with B.new. Even in that case, calling $b.x will still lead to the method defined in the derived class.

```
my A $b = B.new;
$b.x; # B.x
$b.y; # A.y
```

Meta-methods (which also are available for every object without writing any code) provide information about the class details. In particular, to see the exact order in which method resolution will be executed, call the .^mro metamethod.

```
say $b.^mro;
```

In our example, the following order will be printed.

```
((B) (A) (Any) (Mu))
```

Of course, you may call the .^mro method on any other variable or object in a programme, regardless of whether it is an instance of the user-defined class, a simple variable, or a constant. Just get an idea of how this is implemented internally.

```
$ perl6 -e'42.^mro.say'
((Int) (Cool) (Any) (Mu))
```

Multiple inheritance

When more than one class is mentioned in the list of base classes, we have multiple inheritance.

```
class A {
    method a {
        say "A.a"
    }
}

class B {
    method b {
        say "B.b";
    }
}

class C is A is B {
}

my $c = C.new;
$c.a;
$c.b;
```

With multiple inheritance, method resolution order is more important, as different base classes may have methods with the same name, or, for example, the two base classes have another common parent. This is why you should know the order of the base class now.

```
class A {
    method meth {
        say "A.meth"
    }
}

class B {
    method meth {
        say "B.meth";
    }
}
```

```
class C is A is B {
}

class D is B is A {
}
```

Here, the method named meth exists in both parent classes A and B, thus calling it on variables of the types C and D will be resolved differently.

```
my $c = C.new;
$c.meth;  # A.meth

my $d = D.new;
$d.meth;  # B.meth
```

This behaviour is confirmed by the method resolution order list, which is actually used by the compiler.

```
$c.^mro.say;  # ((C) (A) (B) (Any) (Mu))
$d.^mro.say;  # ((D) (B) (A) (Any) (Mu))
```

Private (closed) methods

Now, after we have discussed inheritance, let us return to the private (or closed) methods. These methods may only be used within the class itself. Thus, you cannot call them from the programme that uses an instance of the class. Nor are they accessible in the derived classes. An exclamation mark is used to denote a private method.

The following example demonstrates the usage of a private method of a class. The comments in the code will help you to understand how it works.

```
class A {
    # Method is only available within A
    method !private {
        say "A.private";
    }

    # Public method calling a private method
    method public {
        # You cannot avoid self here.
        # Consider the '!' as a separator like '.'
        self!private;
    }
}

class B is A {
    method method {
        # Again self, but this the '.' this time.
        # This is a public method.
        self.public;

        # This will be a compile-time error.
        # self!private;
    }
}

my $b = B.new;
$b.method;  # A.private
```

The exclamation mark is actually part of the method name. So you can have both method `meth` and method `!meth` in the same class. To access them, use `self.meth` and `self!meth`, respectively:

```
class C {
    method meth  {say 'meth' }
    method !meth {say '!meth'}
    method demo {
        self.meth;
        self!meth;
    }
}

my $c = C.new;
$c.demo;  # Prints both meth and !meth
```

Submethods

Perl 6 defines the so-called submethods for classes. These are the methods which are not propagating to the subclass's definition. The submethods may be either private or public, but they will not be inherited by the children.

```
class A {
    submethod submeth {
        say "A.submeth"
    }
}

class B is A {
}

my A $a;
my B $b;

$a.submeth;    # OK
# $b.submeth;  # Error: No such method 'submeth' for invocant of type 'B'
```

Constructors

You may have noticed in the previous examples that two different approaches to creating a typed variable were used.

The first was via an explicit call of the new constructor. In this case, a new instance was created.

```
my $a = A.new;
```

In the second, a variable was declared as a typed variable. Here, a container was created.

```
my A $a;
```

Creating a container means not only that the variable will be allowed to host an object of that class but also that you will still need to create that object itself.

```
my A $a = A.new;
```

Let us consider an example of a class which involves one public method and one public data field.

```
class A {
    has $.x = 42;
    method m {
        say "A.m";
    }
}
```

The internal public variable $.x is initialized with the constant value.

Now, let us create a scalar container for the variable of the A class.

```
my A $a;
```

The container is here, and we know its type, but there are no data yet. At this moment, the class method may be called. It will work, as it is a class method and does not require any instance with real data.

```
$a.m;  # Prints "A.m"
```

Meanwhile, the $.x field is not available yet.

```
say $a.x;  # Error: Cannot look up attributes in a A type object
```

We need to create an instance object by calling a constructor first.

```
my A $b = A.new;
say $b.x;  # Prints 42
```

Please note that the initialization (= **42**) only happens when a constructor is called. Prior to this, there is no object, and thus no value can be assigned to an attribute.

The **new** method is inherited from the **Mu** class. It accepts a list of the named arguments. So, this method can be used on any object with any reasonable arguments. For instance:

```
my A $c = A.new(x => 14);
say $c.x;  # 14, not 42
```

Note that the name of the field (x) may not be quoted. An attempt of **A.new('x' => 14)** will fail because it will be interpreted as a **Pair** being passed as a positional parameter.

Alternatively, you can use the **:named(value)** format for specifying named parameters:

```
my A $c = A.new :x(14);  # Or A.new(:x(14)) if you wish
say $c.x;  # 14
```

For the more sophisticated constructors, the class's own **BUILD** submethod may be defined. This method expects to get a list of the named arguments.

```
class A {
    # Two fields in an object.
    # One of them will be calculated in the constructor.
    has $.str;
    has $!len;

    # The constructor expects its argument named 'str'.
    submethod BUILD(:$str) {
        # This field is being copied as is:
        $!str = $str;

        # And this field is calculated:
        $!len = $str.chars;
    }
```

```
method dump {
    # Here, we print the current values.
    # The variables are interpolated as usual
    # but to escape an apostrophe character from
    # the variable name, a pair of braces is added.
    "{$.str}'s length is $!len.".say;
    }
}

my $a = A.new(str => "Perl");
$a.dump;
```

This programme prints the following output:

```
Perl's length is 4.
```

Roles

Apart from the bare classes, the Perl 6 language allows roles. These are what are sometimes called interfaces in other object-oriented languages. Both the methods and the data, which are defined in a role, are available for "addition" (or mixing-in) to a new class with the help of the does keyword.

A role looks like a base class that appends its methods and data to generate a new type. The difference between prepending a role and deriving a class from a base class is that with a role, you do not create any inheritance. Instead, all the fields from the role become the fields of an existing class. In other words, classes are the *is a* characteristic of an object, while roles are the *does* traits. With roles, name conflicts will be found at compile time; there is no need to traverse the method resolution order paths.

The following example defines a role, which is later used to create two classes; we could achieve the same with bare inheritance, though:

```
# The role of the catering place is to take orders
# (via the order method), to count the total amount
# of the order (method calc) and issuing a bill (method bill).
role FoodService {
    has @!orders;

    method order($price) {
        @!orders.push($price);
    }

    method calc {
        # [+] is a hyperoperator (hyperop) connecting all the
        # elements of an array.
        # It means that [+] @a is equivalent to
        # @a[0] + @a[1] + ... + @a[N].
        return [+] @!orders;
    }

    method bill {
        # Order's total is still a sum of the orders.
        return self.calc;
    }
}

# Launching a cafe. A cafe is a catering place.
class Cafe does FoodService {
    method bill {
        # But with a small surcharge.
        return self.calc * 1.1;
    }
}

# And now a restaurant.
class Restaurant does FoodService {
    method bill {
        # First, let the customer wait some time.
        sleep 10.rand;

        # Second, increase the prices even more.
        return self.calc * 1.3;
    }
}
```

Let us try that in action. First, the cafe.

```
my $cafe = Cafe.new;
$cafe.order(10);
$cafe.order(20);
say $cafe.bill;  # Immediate 33
```

Then, the restaurant. (Note that this code will have a delay because of the class definition).

```
my $restaurant = Restaurant.new;
$restaurant.order(100);
$restaurant.order(200);
say $restaurant.bill;  # 390 after some unpredictable delay
```

Roles can be used for defining and API and forcing the presence of a method in a class that uses a role. For example, let's create a role named Liquid, which requires that the flows method must be implemented.

```
role Liquid {
    method flows {...}
}

class Water does Liquid {
}
```

It is not possible to run this programme as it generates a compile-time error:

```
Method 'flows' must be implemented by Water because it is
required by a role
```

Note that the ellipsis ... is a valid Perl 6 construction that is used to create forward declarations.

Chapter 5
New Concepts

Channels

Perl 6 includes a number of solutions for parallel and concurrent calculations. The great thing is that this is already built-in into the language and no external libraries are required.

The idea of the channels is simple. You create a channel through which you can read and write. It is a kind of a pipe that can also easily transfer Perl 6 objects. If you are familiar with channels in, for example, Go, you would find Perl 6's channels easily to understand.

Read and write

In Perl 6, there is a predefined class Channel, which includes, among the others, the send and the receive methods. Here is the simplest example, where an integer number first is being sent to the channel $c and is then immediately read from it.

```
my $c = Channel.new;
$c.send(42);
say $c.receive;  # 42
```

A channel can be passed to a sub as any other variable. Should you do that, you will be able to read from that channel in the sub.

```
my $ch = Channel.new;
$ch.send(2017);
func($ch);

sub func($ch) {
    say $ch.receive;  # 2017
}
```

It is possible to send more than one value to a channel. Of course, you can later read them all one by one in the same order as they were sent.

```
my $channel = Channel.new;

# A few even numbers are sent to the channel.
for <1 3 5 7 9> {
    $channel.send($_);
}

# Now, we read the numbers until the channel has them.
# "while @a -> $x" creates a loop with the $x as a loop variable.
while $channel.poll -> $x {
    say $x;
}

# After the last available number, Nil is returned.
$channel.poll.say;  # Nil
```

In the last example, instead of the previously used `receive` method, another one is used: `$channel.poll`. The difference lies in how they handle the end of the queue. When there are no more data in the channel, the `receive` will block the execution of the programme until new data arrive. Instead, the `poll` method returns `Nil` when no data are left.

To prevent the programme from hanging after the channel data is consumed, close the channel by calling the `close` method.

```
$channel.close;
while $channel.receive -> $x {
    say $x;
}
```

Now, you only read data, which are already in the channel, but after the queue is over, an exception will occur: `Cannot receive a message on a closed channel`. Thus either put a `try` block around it or use `poll`.

```
$channel.close;
try {
    while $channel.receive -> $x {
        say $x;
    }
}
```

Here, closing a channel is a required to quit after the last data piece from the channel arrives.

The `list` method

The `list` method accompanies the previously seen methods and returns everything that is left unread in the channel.

```
my $c = Channel.new;

$c.send(5);
$c.send(6);

$c.close;
say $c.list; # (5 6)
```

The method blocks the programme until the channel is open, thus it is wise to close it before calling the `list` method.

Beyond scalars

Channels may also transfer both arrays and hashes and do it as easily as they work with scalars. Unlike Perl 5, an array will not be unfolded to a list of scalars but will be passed as a single unit. Thus, you may write the following code.

```
my $c = Channel.new;
my @a = (2, 4, 6, 8);
$c.send(@a);

say $c.receive; # [2 4 6 8]
```

The @a array is sent to the channel as a whole and later is consumed as a whole with a single `receive` call.

What's more, if you save the received value into a scalar variable, that variable will contain an array.

```
my $x = $c.receive;
say $x.WHAT;  # (Array)
```

The same discussions apply to hashes.

```
my $c = Channel.new;
my %h = (alpha => 1, beta => 2);
$c.send(%h);
```

```
say $c.receive;  # {alpha => 1, beta => 2}
```

Instead of calling the list method, you can use the channel in the list context (but do not forget to close it first).

```
$c.close;
my @v = @$c;
say @v;  # [{alpha => 1, beta => 2}]
```

Note that if you send a list, you will receive it as a list element of the @v array.

Here is another example of "dereferencing" a channel:

```
$c.close;
for @$c -> $x {
    say $x;
}  # {alpha => 1, beta => 2}
```

The closed method
The Channel class also defines a method that checks on whether the channel is closed. This method is called closed.

```
my $c = Channel.new;
say "open" if !$c.closed;  # is open
```

```
$c.close;
say "closed" if $c.closed;  # closed
```

Despite the simplicity of using the method, it in fact returns not a simple Boolean value but a promise object (a variable of the `Promise` class). A promise (we will talk about this later) can be either kept or broken. Thus, if the channel is open, the `closed` promise is not yet kept; it is only given (or planned).

Promise.new(status => PromiseStatus::Planned, ...)

After the channel is closed, the promise is kept.

Promise.new(status => PromiseStatus::Kept, ...)

You can see the state of the promise above in its `status` field.

* * *

In this section, we discussed the simplest applications of channels, where things happen in the same thread. The big thing about channels is that they transparently do the right thing if you're sending in one or more threads, and receiving in another one or more threads. No value will be received by more than one thread, and no value shall be lost because of race conditions when sending them from more than one thread.

Promises

Promises are objects aimed to help synchronize parallel processes. The simplest use case involving them is to notify if the earlier given promise is kept or broken or if its status is not yet known.

Basics

The `Promise.new` constructor builds a new promise. The status of it can be read using the `status` method. Before any other actions are done with the promise, its status remains to be `Planned`.

```
my $p = Promise.new;
say $p.status; # Planned
```

When the promise is kept, call the `keep` method to update the status to the value of `Kept`.

```
my $p = Promise.new;
$p.keep;
say $p.status; # Kept
```

Alternatively, to break the promise, call the `break` method and set the status of the promise to `Broken`.

```
my $p = Promise.new;
say $p.status; # Planned

$p.break;
say $p.status; # Broken
```

Instead of asking for a status, the whole promise object can be converted to a Boolean value. There is the `Bool` method for that; alternatively, the unary operator `?` can be used instead.

```
say $p.Bool;
say ?$p;
```

Keep in mind that as a Boolean value can only take one of the two possible states, the result of the Boolean typecast is not a full replacement for the status method.

There is another method for getting a result called result. It returns truth if the promise has been kept.

```
my $p = Promise.new;
$p.keep;
say $p.result;  # True
```

Be careful. If the promise is not kept at the moment the result is called, the programme will be blocked until the promise is not in the Planned status anymore.

In the case of the broken promise, the call of result throws an exception.

```
my $p = Promise.new;
$p.break;
say $p.result;
```

Run this programme and get the exception details in the console.

Tried to get the result of a broken Promise

To avoid quitting the programme under an exception, surround the code with the try block (but be ready to lose the result of say—it will not appear on the screen).

```
my $p = Promise.new;
$p.break;
try {
    say $p.result;
}
```

The `cause` method, when called instead of the `result`, will explain the details for the broken promise. The method cannot be called on the kept promise:

Can only call cause on a broken promise (status: Kept)

Like with exceptions, both kept and broken promises can be attributed to a message or an object. In this case, the `result` will return that message instead of a bare `True` or `False`.

This is how a message is passed for the kept promise:

```
my $p = Promise.new;
$p.keep('All done');
say $p.status; # Kept
say $p.result; # All done
```

This is how it works with the broken promise:

```
my $p = Promise.new;
$p.break('Timeout');
say $p.status; # Broken
say $p.cause;  # Timeout
```

Factory methods

There are a few factory methods defined in the `Promise` class.

start

The `start` method creates a promise containing a block of code. There is an alternative way to create a promise by calling `Promise.start` via the `start` keyword.

```
my $p = start {
    42
}
```

(Note that in Perl 6, a semicolon is assumed after a closing brace at the end of a line.)

The `start` method returns a promise. It will be broken if the code block throws an exception. If there are no exceptions, the promise will be kept.

```
my $p = start {
    42
}
say $p.result;  # 42
say $p.status;  # Kept
```

Please note that the `start` instruction itself just creates a promise and the code from the code block will be executed on its own. The `start` method immediately returns, and the code block runs in parallel. A test of the promise status will depend on whether the code has been executed or not. Again, remember that `result` will block the execution until the promise is not in the `Planned` status anymore.

In the given example, the `result` method returns the value calculated in the code block. After that, the `status` call will print `Kept`.

If you change the last two lines in the example, the result may be different. To make the test more robust, add a delay within the code block.

```
my $p = start {
    sleep 1;
    42
}
say $p.status;  # Planned
say $p.result;  # 42
say $p.status;  # Kept
```

Now, it can be clearly seen that the first call of `$p.status` is happening immediately after the promise has been created and informs us that the promise is `Planned`. Later, after the `result` unblocked the programme flow in about a second, the second call of `$p.status` prints `Kept`, which means that the execution of the code block is completed and no exceptions were thrown.

104

Would the code block generate an exception, the promise becomes broken.

```
my $p = start {
    die;
}
try {
    say $p.result;
}
say $p.status;  # This line will be executed
                # and will print 'Broken'
```

The second thing you have to know when working with start is to understand what exactly causes an exception. For example, an attempt to divide by zero will only throw an exception when you try using the result of that division. The division itself is harmless. In Perl 6, this behaviour is called *soft failure*. Before the result is actually used, Perl 6 assumes that the result is of the Rat (rational) type.

```
# $p1 is Kept
my $p1 = start {
    my $inf = 1 / 0;
}

# $p2 is Broken
my $p2 = start {
    my $inf = 1 / 0;
    say $inf;
}

sleep 1;  # Wait to make sure the code blocks are done

say $p1.status;  # Kept
say $p2.status;  # Broken
```

in and at

The other two factory methods, Promise.in and Promise.at, create a promise, which will be kept after a given number of seconds or by a given time. For example:

```
my $p = Promise.in(3);

for 1..5 {
    say $p.status;
    sleep 1;
}
```

The programme prints the following lines.

```
Planned
Planned
Planned
Kept
Kept
```

That means that the promise was kept after three seconds.

anyof and allof

Another pair of factory methods, `Promise.anyof` and `Promise.allof`, creates new promises, which will be only kept when at least one of the promises (in the case of `anyof`) is kept or, in the case of `allof`, all of the promises listed at the moment of creation are kept.

One of the useful examples found in the documentation is a timeout keeper to prevent long calculations from hanging the programme.

Create the promise `$timeout`, which must be kept after a few seconds, and the code block, which will be running for longer time. Then, list them both in the constructor of `Promise.anyof`.

```
my $code = start {
    sleep 5
}
my $timeout = Promise.in(3);

my $done = Promise.anyof($code, $timeout);
say $done.result;
```

The code should be terminated after three seconds. At this moment, the $timeout promise is kept, and that makes the $done promise be kept, too.

then

The then method, when called on an already existing promise, creates another promise, whose code will be called after the "parent" promise is either kept or broken.

```
my $p = Promise.in(2);
my $t = $p.then({say "OK"}); # Prints this in two seconds

say "promised"; # Prints immediately
sleep 3;

say "done";
```

The code above produces the following output:

```
promised
OK
done
```

In another example, the promise is broken.

```
Promise.start({    # A new promise
    say 1 / 0      # generates an exception
                   # (the result of the division is used in say).
}).then({          # The code executed after the broken line.
    say "oops"
}).result          # This is required so that we wait until
                   # the result is known.
```

The only output here is the following:

```
oops
```

An example

Finally, a funny example of how promises can be used for implementing the *sleep sort* algorithm. In sleep sort, every integer number, consumed from the input, creates a delay proportional to its value. As the sleep is over, the number is printed out.

Promises are exactly the things that will execute the code and tell the result after they are done. Here, a list of promises is created, and then the programme waits until all of them are done (this time, we do it using the `await` keyword).

```
my @promises;
for @*ARGS -> $a {
    @promises.push(start {
        sleep $a;
        say $a;
    })
}

await(|@promises);
```

Provide the programme with a list of integers:

```
$ perl6 sleep-sort.pl 3 7 4 9 1 6 2 5
```

For each value, a separate promise will be created with a respective delay in seconds. You may experiment and make smaller delays such as `sleep $a / 10` instead. The presence of `await` ensures that the programme is not finished until all the promises are kept.

As an exercise, let's simplify the code and get rid of an explicit array that collects the promises.

```
await do for @*ARGS {
    start {
        sleep $_;
        say $_;
    }
}
```

108

First, we use the $_ variable here and thus don't have to declare $a. Second, notice the do for combination, which returns the result of each loop iteration. The following code will help you to understand how that works:

```
my @a = do for 1..5 {$_ * 2};
say @a;  # [2 4 6 8 10]
```

Chapter 6
Regexes and Grammars

Grammars in Perl 6 are the "next level" of the well-known regular expressions. Grammars let you create much more sophisticated text parsers. A new domain-specific language (DSL), language translator, or interpreter can be created without any external help, using only the facilities that Perl 6 offers with grammars.

Regexes

In fact, Perl 6 just calls regular expressions *regexes*. The basic syntax is a bit different from Perl 5, but most elements (such as quantifiers * or +) still look familiar. The `regex` keyword is used to build a regex. Let us create a regex for the short names of weekdays.

```
my regex weekday
    {[Mon | Tue | Wed | Thu | Fri | Sat | Sun]};
```

The square brackets are enclosing the list of alternatives.

You can use the named regex inside other regexes by referring to its name in a pair of angle brackets. To match the string against a regex, use the *smartmatch* operator (~~).

```
say 'Thu' ~~ m/<weekday>/;
say 'Thy' ~~ m/<weekday>/;
```

These two matches will print the following.

```
「Thu」
  weekday => 「Thu」
False
```

The result of matching is an object of the `Match` type. When you print it, you will see the matched substring inside small square brackets 「...」 .

Regexes are the simplest named constructions. Apart from that, rules and tokens exist (and thus, the keywords `rule` and `token`).

Tokens are different from rules first regarding how they handle *whitespaces*. In rules, whitespaces are part of the regexes. In tokens, whitespaces are just visual separators. We will see more about this in the examples below.

```
my token number_token { <[\d]> <[\d]> }
my rule number_rule { <[\d]> <[\d]> }
```

(Note that there is no need in semicolons after the closing brace.)

The `<[...]>` construction creates a character class. In the example above, the two-character string `42` matches with the `number_token` token but not with the `number_rule` rule.

```
say 1 if "42" ~~ /<number_token>/;
say 1 if "4 2" ~~ /<number_rule>/;
```

The $/ object

As we have just seen, the smartmatch operator comparing a string with a regex returns an object of the `Match` type. This object is stored in the `$/` variable. It also contains all the matching substrings. To keep (catch) the substring a pair of parentheses is used. The first match is indexed as `0`, and you may access it as an array element either using the full syntax `$/[0]` or the shortened one: `$0`.

Remember that even the separate elements like `$0` or `$0` still contain objects of the `Match` type. To cast them to strings or numbers, coercion syntax can be used. For example, `~$0` converts the object to a string, and `+$0` converts it to an integer.

```
'Wed 15' ~~ /(\w+) \s (\d+)/;
say ~$0;  # Wed
say +$1;  # 15
```

Grammars

Grammars are the development of regular expressions. Syntactically, the grammar is defined similar to a class but using the keyword grammar. Inside, it contains tokens and rules. In the next section, we will be exploring the grammar in the examples.

Simple parser

The first example of the grammar application is on grammar for tiny language that defines an assignment operation and contains the printing instruction. Here is an example of a programme in this language.

```
x = 42;
y = x;
print x;
print y;
print 7;
```

Let's start writing the grammar for the language. First, we have to express the fact that a programme is a sequence of statements separated by a semicolon. Thus, at the top level the grammar looks like this:

```
grammar Lang {
    rule TOP {
        ^ <statements> $
    }
    rule statements {
        <statement>+ %% ';'
    }
}
```

Here, Lang is the name of the grammar, and TOP is the initial rule from which the parsing will be started. The rule's content is a regex surrounded by with a pair of symbols, ^ and $, to tie the rule to the beginning and the end of the text. In other words, the whole programme should match the TOP rule. The central part of the rule, <statements>, refers to another rule. Rules will ignore all the spaces between their parts. Thus, you may freely add spaces to the grammar definition to make it easily readable.

The second rule explains the meaning of statements. The statements block is a sequence of separate statements. It should contain at least one statement, as the + quantifier requires, and the delimiter character is a semicolon. The separator is mentioned after the %% symbol. In grammar, this means that you must have the separator character between instructions, but you can omit it after the last one. If there's only one percent character instead of two, the rule will also require the separator after the last statement.

The next step is to describe the statement. At the moment, our language has only two operations: assignment and printing. Each of them accepts either a value or a variable name.

```
rule statement {
    | <assignment>
    | <printout>
}
```

The vertical bar separates alternative branches like it does in regular expressions in Perl 5. To make the code a bit better-looking and simplify the maintenance, an extra vertical bar may be added before the first subrule. The following two descriptions are identical:

```
rule statement {
      <assignment>
    | <printout>
}
rule statement {
    | <assignment>
    | <printout>
}
```

Then, let us define what do `assignment` and `printout` mean.

```
rule assignment {
    <identifier> '=' <expression>
}
rule printout {
    'print' <expression>
}
```

Here, we see literal strings, namely, `'='` and `'print'`. Again, the spaces around them do not affect the rule.

An `expression` matches with either an identifier (which is a variable name in our case) or with a constant value. Thus, an `expression` is either an `identifier` or a `value` with no additional strings.

```
rule expression {
    | <identifier>
    | <value>
}
```

At this point, we should write the rules for identifiers and values. It is better to use another method, named `token`, for that kind of the grammar bit. In tokens, the spaces matter (except for those that are adjacent to the braces).

An identifier is a sequence of letters:

```
token identifier {
    <:alpha>+
}
```

Here, `<:alpha>` is a predefined character class containing all the alphabetical characters.

A value in our example is a sequence of digits, so we limit ourselves to integers only.

```
token value {
    \d+
}
```

Our first grammar is complete. It is now possible to use it to parse a text file.

```
my $parsed = Lang.parsefile('test.lang');
```

If the file content is already in a variable, you may use the Lang.parse($str) method to parse it. (There is more about reading from files in the Appendix.)

If the parsing was successful, that if the file contains a valid programme, the $parse variable will contain an object of the Match type. It is possible to dump it (say $parsed) and see what's there.

```
⌜x = 42;
y = x;
print x;
print y;
print 7;
⌟
 statements => ⌜x = 42;
y = x;
print x;
print y;
print 7;
⌟
   statement =>  ⌜x = 42⌟
    assignment =>  ⌜x = 42⌟
     identifier =>  ⌜x⌟
     expression =>  ⌜42⌟
      value =>  ⌜42⌟
   statement =>  ⌜y = x⌟
    assignment =>  ⌜y = x⌟
     identifier =>  ⌜y⌟
     expression =>  ⌜x⌟
      identifier =>  ⌜x⌟
   statement =>  ⌜print x⌟
```

```
   printout  =>   ⌜print x⌟
     expression  =>   ⌜x⌟
       identifier  =>   ⌜x⌟
   statement  =>   ⌜print y⌟
     printout  =>   ⌜print y⌟
       expression  =>   ⌜y⌟
         identifier  =>   ⌜y⌟
   statement  =>   ⌜print 7⌟
     printout  =>   ⌜print 7⌟
       expression  =>   ⌜7⌟
         value  =>   ⌜7⌟
```

This output corresponds to the sample programme from the beginning of this section. It contains the structure of the parsed programme. The captured parts are displayed in the brackets ⌜...⌟ . First, the whole matched text is printed. Indeed, as the TOP rule uses the pair of anchors ^ ... $, and so the whole text should match the rule.

Then, the parse tree is printed. It starts with the <statements>, and then the other parts of the grammar are presented in full accordance with what the programme in the file contains. On the next level, you can see the content of both the identifier and value tokens.

If the programme is grammatically incorrect, the parsing methods will return an empty value (Any). The same will happen if only the initial part of the programme matches the rules.

Here is the whole grammar for your convenience:

```
grammar Lang {
    rule TOP {
        ^ <statements> $
    }
    rule statements {
        <statement>+ %% ';'
    }
    rule statement {
        | <assignment>
        | <printout>
    }
    rule assignment {
        <identifier> '=' <expression>
    }
    rule printout {
        'print' <expression>
    }
    rule expression {
        | <identifier>
        | <value>
    }
    token identifier {
        <:alpha>+
    }
    token value {
        \d+
    }
}
```

An interpreter

So far, the grammar sees the structure of the programme and can tell if it is grammatically correct, but it does not execute any instructions contained in the programme. In this section, we will extend the parser so that it can actually execute the programme.

Our sample language uses variables and integer values. The values are constants and describe themselves. For the variables, we need to create a storage. In the simplest case, all the variables are global, and a single hash is required: `my %var;`.

The first action that we will implement now, is an assignment. It will take the value and save it in the variable storage. In the `assignment` rule in the grammar, an `expression` is expected on the right side of the equals sign. An expression can be either a variable or a number. To simplify the variable name lookup, let's make the grammar a bit more complicated and split the rules for assignments and printing out into two alternatives.

```
rule assignment {
    | <identifier> '=' <value>
    | <identifier> '=' <identifier>
}
rule printout {
    | 'print' <value>
    | 'print' <identifier>
}
```

Actions

The grammars in Perl 6 allow actions in response to the rule or token matching. Actions are code blocks that are executed when the corresponding rule or token is found in the parsed text. Actions receive an object $/, where you can see the details of the match. For example, the value of $<identifier> will contain an object of the Match type with the information about the substring that actually was consumed by the grammar.

```
rule assignment {
    | <identifier> '=' <value>
        {say "$<identifier>=$<value>"}
    | <identifier> '=' <identifier>
}
```

If you update the grammar with the action above and run the programme against the same sample file, then you will see the substring *x=42* in the output.

120

The Match objects are converted to strings when they are interpolated in double quotes as in the given example: "$<identifier>=$<value>". To use the text value from outside the quoted string, you should make an explicit typecast:

```
rule assignment {
    | <identifier> '=' <value>
        {%var{~$<identifier>} = +$<value>}
    | <identifier> '=' <identifier>
}
```

So far, we've got an action for assigning a value to a variable and can process the first line of the file. The variable storage will contain the pair {x => 42}.

In the second alternative of the assignment rule, the <identifier> name is mentioned twice; that is why you can reference it as to an array element of $<identifier>.

```
rule assignment {
    | <identifier> '=' <value>
    {
        %var{~$<identifier>} = +$<value>
    }
    | <identifier> '=' <identifier>
    {
        %var{~$<identifier>[0]} =
        %var{~$<identifier>[1]}
    }
}
```

This addition to the code makes it possible to parse an assignment with two variables: y = x. The %var hash will contain both values: {x => 42, y => 42}.

Alternatively, capturing parentheses may be used. In this case, to access the captured substring, use special variables, such as $0:

```
rule assignment {
    | (<identifier>) '=' (<value>)
      {
          %var{$0} = +$1
      }
    | (<identifier>) '=' (<identifier>)
      {
          %var{$0} = %var{$1}
      }
}
```

Here, the unary ~ is no longer required when the variable is used as a hash key, but the unary + before $1 is still needed to convert the Match object to a number.

Similarly, create the actions for printing.

```
rule printout {
    | 'print' <value>
      {
          say +$<value>
      }
    | 'print' <identifier>
      {
          say %var{$<identifier>}
      }
}
```

Now, the grammar is able to do all the actions required by the language design, and it will print the requested values:

```
42
42
7
```

As soon as we used capturing parentheses in the rules, the parse tree will contain entries named as 0 and 1, together with the named strings, such as identifier. You can clearly see it when parsing the y = x string:

```
statement =>  「y = x」
 assignment =>  「y = x」
  0 =>  「y」
   identifier =>  「y」
  1 =>  「x」
   identifier =>  「x」
```

An updated parser looks like this:

```
my %var;

grammar Lang {
    rule TOP {
        ^ <statements> $
    }
    rule statements {
        <statement>+ %% ';'
    }
    rule statement {
        | <assignment>
        | <printout>
    }
    rule assignment {
        | (<identifier>) '=' (<value>)
          {
              %var{$0} = +$1
          }
        | (<identifier>) '=' (<identifier>)
          {
              %var{$0} = %var{$1}
          }
    }
    rule printout {
        | 'print' <value>
          {
              say +$<value>
          }
        | 'print' <identifier>
          {
              say %var{$<identifier>}
          }
    }
```

```
    token identifier {
        <:alpha>+
    }
    token value {
        \d+
    }
}

Lang.parsefile('test.lang');
```

For convenience, it is possible to put the code of actions in a separate class. This helps a lot when the actions are more complex and contain more than one or two lines of code.

To create an external action, create a class, which will later be referenced via the :actions parameter upon the call of the parse or parsefile methods of the grammar. As with built-in actions, the actions in an external class receive the $/ object of the Match type.

First, we will train on a small isolated example and then return to our custom language parser.

```
grammar G {
    rule TOP {^ \d+ $}
}

class A {
    method TOP($/) {say ~$/}
}

G.parse("42", :actions(A));
```

Both the grammar G and the action class A have a method called TOP. The common name connects the action with the corresponding rule. When the grammar parses the provided test string and consumes the value of 42 by the ^ \d $ rule, the A::TOP action is triggered, and the $/ argument is passed to it, which is immediately printed.

AST and attributes

Now, we are ready to simplify the grammar again after we split the as-signment and printout rules into two alternatives each. The difficulty was that without the split, it was not possible to understand which branch had been triggered. You either needed to read the value from the value token or get the name of the variable from the identifier token and look it up in the variable storage.

Perl 6's grammars offer a great mechanism that is common in language parsing theory, the abstract syntax tree, shortened as AST.

First of all, update the rules and remove the alternatives from some of them. The only rule containing two branches is the expression rule.

```
rule assignment {
    <identifier> '=' <expression>
}
rule printout {
    'print' <expression>
}
rule expression {
    | <identifier>
    | <value>
}
```

The syntax tree that is built during the parse phase can contain the re-sults of the calculations in the previous steps. The Match object has a field ast, dedicated especially to keep the calculated values on each node. It is possible to simply read the value to get the result of the previously completed actions. The tree is called abstract because how the value is calculated is not very important. What is important is that when the action is triggered, you have a single place with the result you need to complete an action.

The action can save its own result (and thus pass it further on the tree) by calling the $/.make method. The data you save there are accessible via the made field, which has the synonym ast.

Let's fill the attribute of the syntax tree for the `identifier` and `value` tokens. The match with an identifier produces the variable name; when the value is found, the action generates a number. Here are the methods of the actions' class.

```
method identifier($/) {
    $/.make(~$0);
}
method value($/) {
    $/.make(+$0);
}
```

Move one step higher, where we build the value of the expression. It can be either a variable value or an integer.

As the `expression` rule has two alternatives, the first task will be to understand which one matches. For that, check the presence of the corresponding fields in the `$/` object.

(If you use the recommended variable name `$/` in the signature of the action method, you may access its fields differently. The full syntax is `$/<identifier>`, but there is an alternative version `$<identifier>`.)

The two branches of the expression method behave differently. For a number, it extracts the value directly from the captured substring. For a variable, it gets the value from the `%var` hash. In both cases, the result is stored in the AST using the `make` method.

```
method expression($/) {
    if $<identifier> {
        $/.make(%var{$<identifier>});
    }
    else {
        $/.make(+$<value>);
    }
}
```

To use the variables that are not yet defined, we can add the defined-or operator to initialise the variable with the zero value.

126

```
$/.make(%var{$<identifier>} // 0);
```

Now, the expression will have a value attributed to it, but the source of the value is not known anymore. It can be a variable value or a constant from the file. This makes the `assignment` and `printout` actions simpler:

```
method printout($/) {
    say $<expression>.ast;
}
```

All you need for printing the value is to get it from the `ast` field.

For the `assignment`, it is a bit more complex but can still be written in a single line.

```
method assignment($/) {
    %var{$<identifier>} = $<expression>.made;
}
```

The method gets the `$/` object and uses the values of its `identifier` and `expression` elements. The first one is converted to the string and becomes the key of the `%var` hash. From the second one, we get the value by fetching the `made` attribute.

Finally, let us stop using the global variable storage and move the hash into the action class (we don't need it in the grammar itself). It thus will be declared as `has %!var;` and used as a private key variable in the body of the actions: `%!var{...}`.

After this change, it is important to create an instance of the actions class before paring it with a grammar:

```
Lang.parsefile(
    'test.lang',
    :actions(LangActions.new())
);
```

Here is the complete code of the parser with actions.

```
grammar Lang {
    rule TOP {
        ^ <statements> $
    }
    rule statements {
        <statement>+ %% ';'
    }
    rule statement {
        | <assignment>
        | <printout>
    }
    rule assignment {
        <identifier> '=' <expression>
    }
    rule printout {
        'print' <expression>
    }
    rule expression {
        | <identifier>
        | <value>
    }
    token identifier {
        (<:alpha>+)
    }
    token value {
        (\d+)
    }
}
```

```
class LangActions {
    has %var;

    method assignment($/) {
        %!var{$<identifier>} = $<expression>.made;
    }
    method printout($/) {
        say $<expression>.ast;
    }
    method expression($/) {
        if $<identifier> {
            $/.make(%!var{$<identifier>} // 0);
        }
        else {
            $/.make(+$<value>);
        }
    }
    method identifier($/) {
        $/.make(~$0);
    }
    method value($/) {
        $/.make(+$0);
    }
}

Lang.parsefile(
    'test.lang',
    :actions(LangActions.new())
);
```

Calculator

When considering language parsers, implementing a calculator is like writing a "Hello, World!" programme. In this section, we will create a grammar for the calculator that can handle the four arithmetical operations and parentheses. The hidden advantage of the calculator example is that you have to teach it to follow the operations priority and nested expressions.

Our calculator grammar will expect the single expression at a top level. The priority of operations will be automatically achieved by the traditional approach to grammar construction, in which the expression consists of terms and factors.

The terms are parts separated by pluses and minuses:

```
<term>+ %% ['+'|'-']
```

Here, Perl 6's %% symbol is used. You may also rewrite the rule using more traditional quantifiers:

```
<term> [['+'|'-'] <term>]*
```

Each term is, in turn, a list of factors separated by the symbols for multiplication or division:

```
<factor>+  %% ['*'|'/']
```

Both terms and factors can contain either a value or a group in parentheses. The group is basically another expression.

```
rule group {
    '(' <expression> ')'
}
```

This rule refers to the expression rule and thus can start another recursion loop.

It's time to introduce the enhancement of the value token so that it accepts the floating point values. This task is easy; it only requires creating a regex that matches the number in as many formats as possible. I will skip the negative numbers and the numbers in scientific notation.

```
token value {
    | \d+['.' \d+]*
    | '.' \d+
}
```

Here is the complete grammar of the calculator:

```
grammar Calc {
    rule TOP {
        ^ <expression> $
    }
    rule expression {
        | <term>+ %% $<op>=(['+'|'-'])
        | <group>
    }
    rule term {
        <factor>+  %% $<op>=(['*'|'/'])
    }
    rule factor {
        | <value>
        | <group>
    }
    rule group {
        '(' <expression> ')'
    }
    token value {
        | \d+['.' \d+]*
        | '.' \d+
    }
}
```

Note the $<op>=(...) construction in some of the rules. This is the named capture. The name simplifies the access to a value via the $/ variable. In this case, you can reach the value as $<op>, and you don't have to worry about the possible change of the variable name after you update a rule as it happens with the numbered variables $0, $1, etc.

Now, create the actions for the compiler. At the TOP level, the rule returns the calculated value, which it takes from the ast field of the expression.

```
class CalcActions {
    method TOP($/) {
        $/.make: $<expression>.ast
    }
    ...
}
```

The actions of the underlying rules `groups` and `value` are as simple as we've just seen.

```
method group($/) {
    $/.make: $<expression>.ast
}

method value($/) {
    $/.make: +$/
}
```

The rest of the actions are a bit more complicated. The `factor` action contains two alternative branches, just as the `factor` rule does.

```
method factor($/) {
    if $<value> {
        $/.make: +$<value>
    }
    else {
        $/.make: $<group>.ast
    }
}
```

Move on to the `term` action. Here, we have to take care of the list with its variable length. The rule's regex has the + quantifier, which means that it can capture one or more elements. Also, as the rule handles both the multiplication and the division operators, the action must distinguish between the two cases. The $<op> variable contains either the * or the / character.

This is how the syntax tree looks like for the string with three terms, 3*4*5:

```
expression =>  「3*4*5」
 term =>  「3*4*5」
  factor =>  「3」
   value =>  「3」
  op =>  「*」
  factor =>  「4」
   value =>  「4」
  op =>  「*」
 factor =>  「5」
  value =>  「5」
```

As you can see, there are factor and op entries on the top levels. You will see the values as $<factor> and $<op> inside the actions. At least one $<factor> will always be available. The values of the nodes will already be known and available in the ast property. Thus, all you need to do is to traverse over the elements of those two arrays and perform either multiplication or division.

```
method term($/) {
    my $result = $<factor>[0].ast;

    if $<op> {
        my @ops = $<op>.map(~*);
        my @vals = $<factor>[1..*].map(*.ast);

        for 0..@ops.elems - 1 -> $c {
            if @ops[$c] eq '*' {
                $result *= @vals[$c];
            }
            else {
                $result /= @vals[$c];
            }
        }
    }

    $/.make: $result;
}
```

In this code fragment, the star character appears in the new role of a placeholder that tells Perl that it should process the data that it can get at this moment. It sounds weird, but it works perfectly and intuitively.

The @ops array with a list of the operation symbols consists of the elements that we got after stringifying the $<op>'s value:

```
my @ops = $<op>.map(~*);
```

The values themselves will land in the @vals array. To ensure that the values of the two arrays, @vals and @ops, correspond to each other, the slice of $<factor> is taken, which starts at the second element:

```
my @vals = $<factor>[1..*].map(*.ast);
```

Finally, the expression action is either to take the calculated value of group or to perform the sequence of additions and subtractions. The algorithm is close to the one of the term's action.

```
method expression($/) {
    if $<group> {
        $/.make: $<group>.ast
    }
    else {
        my $result = $<term>[0].ast;

        if $<op> {
            my @ops = $<op>.map(~*);
            my @vals = $<term>[1..*].map(*.ast);
            for 0..@ops.elems - 1 -> $c {
                if @ops[$c] eq '+' {
                    $result += @vals[$c];
                }
                else {
                    $result -= @vals[$c];
                }
            }
        }
         $/.make: $result;
    }
}
```

The majority of the code for the calculator is ready. Now, we need to read the string from the user, pass it to the parser, and print the result.

```
my $calc = Calc.parse(
            @*ARGS[0],
            :actions(CalcActions)
        );
say $calc.ast;
```

Let's see if it works.

```
$ perl6 calc.pl '39 + 3.14 * (7 - 18 / (505 - 502)) - .14'
42
```

It does.

On github.com/ash/lang, you can find the continuation of the code demonstrated in this chapter, which combines both the language translator and the calculator to allow the user write the arithmetical expressions in the variable assignments and the print instructions. Here is an example of what that interpreter can process:

```
x = 40 + 2;
print x;

y = x - (5/2);
print y;

z = 1 + y * x;
print z;

print 14 - 16/3 + x;
```

Appendix

Unicode

The strings in Perl 6 are internally handled in the format called NFG (Normalization Form Grapheme). From a practical point of view, that means that, for any symbol, you can get its NFC, NFD, NFKC and KFKD forms. I will refer you to read about the details of these formats to the Unicode standard. In simple words, these are different canonical and decomposed forms of a symbol.

There are four methods with those names, and you may call them on character strings:

```
say $s.NFC;  # codepoint
say $s.NFD;
say $s.NFKC;
say $s.NFKD;
```

The full canonical name of a character is returned by the method uniname:

```
say 'λ'.uniname;  # GREEK SMALL LETTER LAMDA
```

In the string class, the encode method is defined; it helps to see how the string is built internally in one of the Unicode charsets:

```
my $name = 'naïve';
say $name.encode('UTF-8');   # utf8:0x<6e 61 c3 af 76 65>
say $name.encode('UTF-16');  # utf16:0x<6e 61 ef 76 65>
```

As an exercise, examine the output for the following characters. The unidump function, shown below, prints some characteristics of the Unicode characters.

```
unidump('אַ');
unidump('ы');
unidump('å');
unidump('é');
```

```
unidump('Ÿ');
# One of the few characters, for which all the four
# canonical forms are different.

unidump('й');
unidump('²');
unidump('Æ');

sub unidump($s) {
    say $s;
    say $s.chars;  # number of graphemes
    say $s.NFC;    # code point
    say $s.NFD;
    say $s.NFKC;
    say $s.NFKD;
    say $s.uniname;  # the Unicode name of the character
    say $s.uniprop;  # the Unicode properties of the first grapheme
    say $s.NFD.list;  # as a list
    say $s.encode('UTF-8').elems;  # number of bytes
    say $s.encode('UTF-16').elems;
    say $s.encode('UTF-8');  # as utf8:0x<...>
    say '';
}
```

The NFKC and NFKD forms, in particular, transform the sub- and superscript to regular digits.

```
say '2'.NFKD;  # NFKD:0x<0032>
say '²'.NFKD;  # NFKD:0x<0032>
```

The `unimatch` function indicates whether a character belongs to one of the Unicode character groups.

```
say unimatch('道', 'CJK');  # True
```

Be warned, because some characters can look the same but are in fact different characters in different parts of the Unicode table.

```
say unimatch('i', 'Cyrillic');  # True
say unimatch('i', 'Cyrillic');  # False
```

The characters in the example are CYRILLIC SMALL LETTER YI and LATIN SMALL LETTER I WITH DIAERESIS, respectively; their NFD representations are 0x<0456 0308> and 0x<0069 0308>.

It is also possible to check the Unicode properties using regexes:

```
say 1 if 'э' ~~ /<:Cyrillic>/;
say 1 if 'э' ~~ /<:Ll>/;  # Letter lowercase
```

Use the uniprop method to get the properties:

```
say "x".uniprop;  # Ll
```

To create a Unicode string directly, you may use the constructor of the Uni class:

```
say Uni.new(0x0439).Str;       # й
say Uni.new(0xcf, 0x94).Str;   # Ï
```

Also, you can embed copepoints in the string:

```
say "\x0439";     # й
say "\xcf\x94";   # Ï
```

Whatever (*)

In Perl 6, the star character * can be associated with one of the prede-fined classes, Whatever and WhateverCode.

We'll start with an object of the Whatever class.

```
say *.WHAT;  # (Whatever)
```

The construction like 1 .. * creates a Range object, where its upper limit is not fixed to any particular number.

```
say (1 .. *).WHAT; # (Range)
```

Here is an example with a loop that prints the numbers from 5 to 10 line by line:

```
for (5 .. *) {
    .say;
    last if $_ == 10;
}
```

Now, try array indices and ask to take all the elements starting from the fourth one:

```
my @a = <2 4 6 8 10 12>;
say @a[3 .. *]; # (8 10 12)
```

The "three dots" operator in combination with a star creates a sequence.

```
say (1 ... *).WHAT; # (Seq)
```

You can use it when you need a lazy and potentially infinite list. A lazy list is a list whose elements are evaluated only when they are necessary for the execution of the programme.

In the following example, an array does not know its size, but you can read infinitely from it; the lazy list will supply new elements:

```
my @a = (100 ... *);

for (0 .. 5) {
    say "Element $_ is @a[$_]";
}
```

This programme will print five lines corresponding to the first five elements of the @a array, which contain values from 100 to 105, including 105. If you change the range in the for loop from 0 .. 5 to 0 .. *, you will get a programme that prints infinitely.

It is possible to modify the algorithm for generating the new values of the sequence by giving a hint to the compiler:

```
my @a = (1, 2 ... *);      # step by 1
say @a[1..5];              # (2 3 4 5 6)

my @b = (2, 4 ... *);      # even numbers
say @b[1..5];              # (4 6 8 10 12)

my @c = (2, 4, 8 ... *);   # powers of two
say @c[1..5];              # (4 8 16 32 64)
```

Together with a list repetition operator, xx, the Whatever object forms an infinite list containing the same value.

```
my @default_values = 'NULL' xx *;
```

Now, let's move on to the WhateverCode object. It is an anonymous code block, which is a good match for simple functions, such as these:

```
my $f = * ** 2;    # square
say $f(16);        # 256

my $xy = * ** *;   # power of any
say $xy(3, 4);     # 81
```

In Perl 6, the transformation from a code with a star to an anonymous code block is called *whatever-currying*. In the traditional style of programming, you introduce a variable to get the same result. In Perl 6, a compiler creates that for you. The following two examples are equivalent to the two above.

```
# An anonymous code block with one argument $x
my $f = -> $x {$x ** 2};
say $f(16);  # 256
```

```
# A block with two arguments; names are alphabetically sorted
my $xy = {$^a ** $^b};
say $xy(3, 4);  # 81
```

142

Whatever-currying is also happening, for example, when we want to refer to the last elements of an array using negative indices. In the following example, we pick array elements from the fourth to the second-to-last one.

```
my @a = <2 4 6 8 10 12>;
say @a[3 .. *-2]; # (8 10)
```

In Perl 5, you could get the last element of an array with the -1 index. In Perl 6, the access @a[-1] will generate an error:

*Unsupported use of a negative -1 subscript to index from the end; in Perl 6 please use a function such as *-1*

So, you need to add a star:

```
say @a[*-1]; # 12
```

Here, the compiler will convert @a[*-1] into the following code:

```
@a[@a.elems - 1]
```

Another common use case of WhateverCode is to provide a compiler with a rule for generating infinite sequences.

```
my @f = 0, 1, * + * ... *;
say @f[1..7].join(', '); # 1, 1, 2, 3, 5, 8, 13
```

This example creates a lazy list containing the Fibonacci numbers. The * + * construction will be implicitly replaced with something like {$^a + $^b}. Note that the first two stars in the example are part of what will become an anonymous code block, while the last one is a single Whatever object.

Files

To get the content of a file, use the `slurp` built-in function, which reads the whole file and returns a string.

```
say slurp "file.txt";
```

The function that does the opposite is called `spurt`, it writes the string to a file.

Let us implement the Unix's `cp` command in Perl 6.

```
my ($source, $dest) = @*ARGS;

my $data = slurp $source;
spurt $dest, $data;
```

By default, either a new destination file will be created or rewritten if it already exists. You can open the file in the append mode by adding the `:append` value in the third argument:

```
spurt $dest, $data, :append;
```

Another mode, :createonly, generates an error if the file exists.

```
spurt $dest, $data, :createonly;
```

Both `slurp` and `spurt` accept an argument with the encoding name:

```
my ($source, $dest) = @*ARGS;

my $data = slurp $source, enc => 'UTF-8';
spurt $dest, $data, enc => 'UTF-16';
```

The `Str` class inherits (from the `Cool` class) the `IO` method that returns an object of the `IO::Path` class. It contains some useful information about the file.

For example, this is how you can get the absolute path to a local file:

```
say 'file.txt'.IO.abspath;
```

The IO.dir method prints the content of a directory:

```
say '.'.IO.dir;
```

The IO.extension method returns an extension of a file:

```
say $filename.IO.extension;
say $filename.IO.extension;
```

Finally, there are one-letter named methods for making checks of the file's or directory's existence or checking its properties:

```
say 1 if 'file.txt'.IO.e;  # same as -e 'file.txt' in Perl 5 (file exists)
say 1 if 'file.txt'.IO.f;  # -f (is a file)
say 1 if '..'.IO.d;        # -d (is a directory)
```

Programming for the Internet

The simplest way to build a web server in Perl 6 is to use a PSGI server called Bailador. This is a module that you can find on the official page with the list of Perl 6 modules: modules.perl6.org. If you are using the Rakudo Star distribution, use the panda* command line utility to install the module.

```
$ panda install Bailador
```

Bailador copies the interface of the well-known framework Dancer for Perl 5. The name is the same but in Spanish.

---

* At the moment of writing this book, panda was about to become outdated, and the new recommended tool will be zef. Please refer to the documentation of your Perl 6 distribution on how to install modules.

Here is the minimal programme that implements the web server.

```
use Bailador;

get '/' => sub {
    'Hello, world!'
}

baile;
```

The programme describes the action, which the server does in response to the request to its home page. The **baile** (*dance* in Spanish) method starts the main loop of the PSGI server.

Run the programme:

```
$ perl6 web1.pl
```

You will get the output informing you that the server is ready to accept requests.

Entering the development dance floor: http://0.0.0.0:3000
[2016-12-27T20:27:34Z] Started HTTP server.

Open that page in a browser, and you will see the desired output: "Hello, world!"

The next step is to parse the URL and respond accordingly. Bailador allows extract parameters from the URL with the colon syntax:

```
get '/:name' => sub ($name) {
    "Hello, $name!"
}
```

Please note that you cannot omit the space after the **sub** keyword. There is an alternative. As the sub is anonymous, you may use the pointy block instead:

```
get '/:name' => -> $name {
    "Hello, $name!"
}
```

Add it to the programme, restart the server, and go to, for example, http://0.0.0.0:3000/abc. You should get the "Hello, abc" output in the browser.

Bailador is happy to accept regexes instead of the fixed URLs. For example, let's create the URL /square-of/N, where the N can be any non-negative integer.

```
get / 'square-of/' (<digit>+) / => sub ($n) {
    $n * $n
}
```

The regex pattern / 'square-of/' (<digit>+) / contains the capturing part, and so the variable $n will be set to the number from the URL. As Bailador reads the address patterns in the order they appear in the file, make sure to put the method above the handler of /name. Now, test how it works at http://0.0.0.0:3000/square-of/5; it should print 25.

It is possible to access some environment variables in the URL handler. Use the request method and take the request.env hash from it, as is demonstrated in the example:

```
get '/ua' => sub {
    request.env<HTTP_USER_AGENT> ~
    '<br />' ~
    request.env<QUERY_STRING>
}
```

The page http://0.0.0.0:3000/ua?key=value will now print the user agent name and list the query parameters of the request.

After we generate the output from the Perl code, let us move to using templates. Bailador will search for the template files in the views directory.

Save a simple text template to `views/test.tt`, and use it in the server like this:

```
use Bailador;

get '/form' => sub {
    template 'test.tt';
}

baile;
```

To print something inside the template, pass the data in hash:

```
get '/form/:name' => sub ($name) {
    template 'name.tt', {name => $name}
}
```

You can access the data from a template. It receives the argument containing everything that you just passed.

```
% my ($params) = @_;

Hi, <%= $params<name> %>!
```

Database access

Install the DBIish module to get a powerful tool for working with databases[*]:

```
$ panda install DBIish
```

You also will need the database driver; for example, libmysqlclient for working with MySQL. Check the documentation of the DBIish module on modules.perl6.org if you want to work with a different database engine.

---

[*] See the footnote in the previous section regarding the tool for installing modules.

148

The module provides an interface similar to the DBI's in Perl 5. You obtain a database handler, $dbh, and they work via the statement handler, $sth. Let us see some details in the following example.

```
use DBIish;

# Connecting to a remote database
my $dbh = DBIish.connect(
    'mysql',
    :host<example.com>,
    :port(3306),
    :database<test>,
    :user<test>,
    :password<test_password>
);

# Now, prepare the statement to get all the data from a table
my $sth = $dbh.prepare("select * from calendar");
# And execute the request
$sth.execute;

# Fetch all the rows
my @arr = $sth.allrows;
say @arr;

# Finalise the statement and close the connection
$sth.finish;
$dbh.dispose;
```

There are several ways of fetching data. The one shown in the code is the $sth.allrows method that returns a list of lists with the data from the table.

Alternatively, rows can be read one by one using the $sth.row method. To get the row data in a hash, add the :hash attribute: $sth.row(:hash).

```
my $sth = $dbh.prepare("select what, when from calendar");
$sth.execute;

my $row_hash = $sth.row(:hash);
say $row_hash;
```

With the `insert` statements, placeholders may be used to avoid the need of escaping the values before injecting them into the SQL query. In the following example, a new row will be written to the database table. The actual values are passed to the `execute` method.

```
my $sth = $dbh.prepare(
    "insert into calendar values (?, ?)"
);

$sth.execute('2017-01-01', 'Wake up');
```

Conclusion

That's all, folks. We discussed a lot of things and how they work in Perl 6. I hope that this has been a good introduction to the language for you and that you will be able to use it in your new projects.

There are still many topics left. Your starting point for the new bits of information should be the language's official web page, perl6.org. The site contains extensive documentation and many examples.

All the code examples in the book were tested in December 2016 with the *Rakudo Star* compiler, version 2016.11. You can download it from rakudo.org/how-to-get-rakudo. You may also check the small example files from the book in the repository at github.com/ash/perl6-at-a-glance.

Remember that Perl 6 and its compilers are still in development; that means that both the code in this book and in the documentation on the site may work incorrectly or even not compile. If you experience any problems, you are always welcome to ask for advice in the Perl 6 Community (there are a few links at perl6.org/community) or in the *Perl6* group on Facebook.

Regarding the content of the book, contact me directly via e-mail at andy@shitov.ru.

Andrew Shitov
Amsterdam, 28 December 2016